The
No Bullshit
Approach
to
Create the Life You Want

Written by J D Mo'orea

Copyright © 2017 by J D Mo'orea.

All rights reserved. This book or any portion thereof may not be reproduced or used in any manner whatsoever without the express written permission of the publisher except for the use of brief quotations in a book review.

ISBN: 978-0-9872439-1-1

Contents

Acknowledgments	5
Preface	6
Introduction	9
Chapter One: Attitude	15
Chapter Two: Decide	33
Chapter Three: Take Action	43
Chapter Four: Learning & Growth	54
Chapter Five: Wealth	67
Chapter Six: Health	122
Chapter Seven: Love	135
Chapter Eight: Happiness	146
Recommended Reading	175
Quotes	178

Acknowledgments

To all the wonderful mentors and life coaches in the field of personal development, who have inspired and continue to inspire millions of people around the world; I say thank you.

To the leaders in the field of human behaviour, quantum physics and personal development, such as Dr John Demartini, Dr Wayne Dyer, Zig Ziglar, Dr Deepak Chopra, Jim Rohn, Esther and Jerry Hicks, Napoleon Hill, Dale Carnegie, Christopher Howard, Don Tolman and many more; you are raising the consciousness of the world and in turn, improving the lives of millions of people, for generations to follow.

To the exceptional "world beaters" and entrepreneurs, like Richard Branson, Oprah Winfrey, Elon Musk, Nelson Mandela and anyone else who has dared to dream and go against society's beliefs in changing the world; I salute you.

Finally; to the giant of the personal development industry (Both figuratively & literally) and the man who not only created the master that he became himself, but in doing so, changed millions of lives around the world. His teaching of complex things, in the most simplistic way, has allowed many to benefit from his genius; Tony Robbins. You changed my life (With a little help from myself) and you continue to inspire me every single day. You not only have a huge personality (and huge hands), but you have the biggest heart, I have ever witnessed in a human being. You may not be my guru (a play on his 2016 documentary – "I am not your guru"); but you are my hero.

It is on the shoulders of these great men and women that we can stand, in reaching our own goals and leaving our mark on the world.

TO YOU ALL, I SAY THANK YOU

Preface

Let me start by saying congratulations, for taking the first and most important step, towards living a fulfilling life, by searching for something to assist in your journey towards creating the life that you want. The fact that you have even made this small commitment, puts you ahead of 90% of the world's population, who would rather do nothing, than do something to be happier and create abundance in their life.

For this, I applaud you. As you may have gathered by the title of this book, unfortunately, this is where niceties end and reality kicks in. Throughout my life, I've been known to be a straight shooter and someone who does not bullshit, so I'm going to give it to you straight, as only I know how. I do this with much love and in the hope that this is precisely what you need, to kickstart you towards unstoppable momentum, in achieving everything that you desire in life.

From my experience, a good coach or mentor, is someone who tells it as it is, through complete honesty. A person who provides easy to apply strategies to achieving your goals and is supportive and compassionate. Someone who can see your strengths and weaknesses and guide you accordingly.

One of my greatest mentors; Tony Robbins, does precisely this. He is a caring individual and he has great strategies, but he does not fluff around, or blow smoke up your arse. Tony is sort after as a coach, to get results; not to make his clients feel good. They feel good because he gets results; not the other way around. My desire is to provide you, with a similar no-nonsense approach, so that you too, can achieve the life that you want.

Throughout this book, I will share with you some of the tools that I have learnt, as a result of reading over 280 books, attending many seminars and listening to countless hours of podcasts and online videos on personal de-

Preface

velopment. They say that when the student is ready, the teacher will appear, so it is my absolute pleasure to be that teacher for you, by way of this book.

Let's get one thing straight though; this book is <u>not</u> going to change your life. You are not going to finish reading it and suddenly have the life you want, because books are <u>not</u> the answer to changing your life. <u>You</u> are the answer and <u>you</u> are going to change your life. Books are knowledge, but if left unused, that knowledge is a waste. This book is simply going to give you some easy to use tools, that I have learnt myself, which, if used properly, will propel you in the direction you want to go, but unless <u>you</u> take control, then nothing will change.

No book, seminar, university degree, or life coach is going to change your life; only <u>you</u> are. (Got the hint yet?) There is nothing in this book that will fix you, or your life. No magic pill or secret potion will cure everything. Most of what is written in this book, you have probably heard before and if not, you will think "well that's common sense isn't it?" The problem is, that most of us don't use that which is supposed to be so common.

I too had read books, listened to audio series and attended seminars, but couldn't work out why my life hadn't changed. It took me many years to realise, that I was relying on people like Tony Robbins and Dr John Demartini, to give me the easy answer. While these men are incredible mentors, unless I took the bull by the horns (so to speak) and made a commitment to making things happen, my life would never be as amazing as I wished it would be; no matter how good these mentors were.

What I know now and what I want to share with you, is that you are the answer to creating the life you desire. Not me, not Tony or anyone else, but you. The reason I mention this straight off the bat, is because I want you to be ready and in the right frame of mind with a willing attitude, before we go anywhere near the tools that I am going to share with you to create the life you deserve.

This book contains easy to take steps that I have learnt and applied to my own life. These tools can change your life, but only when you take charge of the process. Unless you're going to commit 100% to making the necessary changes and take full responsibility for your own destiny, then you may as well return the book from where you bought it and beg for a refund. The other option, is to use it as a fire starter, because without you deciding and committing to the process, there's no point reading on.

Of all the books that I've read, quite a high number were overwhelming, with the amount of information that they contained. While a "value for money" approach, should be at the heart of any book, for me, it is just as important, that you grasp what information there is in this book, rather than flood you with too much information. I want to make sure that I don't overwhelm you throughout this book and I want to ensure that you use what is listed here, rather than forget most of it.

This book is not a be all and end all of any of the subjects that we touch on. Rather, this book, is the beginning of your new life and just the start of your growth in these areas. I promise you, that if you absorb the information in this book properly, you will be naturally compelled to find more books and information on these topics. As the old saying goes, "give a man a fish and you will feed him for a day. Teach a man to fish and you will feed him for a lifetime".

In the entertainment industry, there is a saying that you should "always leave the audience wanting more." This book, uses the same concept. It's better to spark your interest enough, that you want more and then pursue it, rather than bore you to the point that you forget everything written here. This is not to say that I plan to write another book on these topics; not at all. My hope is that you explore some of the dozens of books that I list at the end of his book, on all of the topics discussed here.

Throughout the book, I touch on many subjects and concepts. To go into great depth, on each one of them, would make this book, as big as a phone book. Each of my recommended books at the end, are a continuation, of the ideas and strategies contained in this book. It is up to you, to choose which ones (or which path), you take. This is your journey, not mine, so while I am helping to facilitate your journey, you are in the driver's seat.

Ok, enough about me banging on about it; let's get started.

Introduction

"A good speech should be like a woman's skirt; long enough to cover the topic and short enough to create interest."
—Winston Churchill

There is a huge misconception, that successful people, who have successful businesses or people who are successful life coaches or authors, are born into that lifestyle. Like they were born with a silver spoon in their mouth, or a wad of one hundred-dollar bills in their backside. The truth of the matter is, that this couldn't be further from the truth. Most of these people are quite the opposite in fact. Almost every truly successful person in history, came from a background that most people would see as a disadvantage. Thankfully, the successful people, saw their situation differently.

For example, Tony Robbins; world famous life strategist, was beaten by his mother as a child and had to endure several step dads, before being kicked out of home at age sixteen. Oprah Winfrey was molested as a young child and gave birth to a child (only to lose it) at age fourteen. Richard Branson was dyslexic. Stevie Wonder was born six weeks premature, which lead to him being permanently blind.

Dr John Demartini; one of the world's leading life coaches, was told he had learning disabilities and ran away from home at seventeen and hitch hiked to Hawaii before almost dying in a tent from malnourishment and possible drug overdose. Dr Wayne Dyer; who is one of the world's greatest spiritual leaders, grew up in several orphanages and foster homes from age three to nine. Albert Einstein didn't speak until he was four years old. Charlize Theron witnessed her mother shoot her father dead when she was fifteen and Andrea Bocelli; one of the greatest singers in history, was blind from the age of twelve.

CREATE THE LIFE YOU WANT

I want to make this point simply, to ensure that while you're reading this, that you don't start telling yourself, that you can't create the life that these people have, because of your own circumstances. These people didn't have the easiest of starts in life, yet they are some of the most successful people in their fields. These people didn't let adversity or hard times dictate their lives. I'd argue that in all of these cases, they used these adversities as motivation, inspiration and as leverage, to create the extraordinary lives that we now know.

Whilst I am by no means trying to put myself in the same category as these incredible role models, I too was not born into a rich family, with a great education, lots of money and lots of opportunities. My family was modest, my education was in public schools and I certainly wasn't a straight "A" student. In fact, once I hit high school, I was more interested in Co-curriculum activities, than traditional school work. Even at that young age, I thought that what the education system was teaching kids, was rubbish; and I was right.

My parents did provide for us and I had what I would consider a normal upbringing, however, the people I called "mum and dad", we're in fact my grandparents. There is nothing too obscure about this, other than the fact that my biological mother was legally my sister. You see, my biological mother was only eighteen when she gave birth to me and my biological father was a truck driver who, for the most part, worked interstate and unbeknownst to my mother, was married to another woman.

In the 1970's in Australia, there was no support from the government for single mothers, so my mother had no other option but to give me up for adoption. Luckily for her, my grandfather suggested that he and my grandmother adopted me. This all sounds straight forward, but it came with the condition that my biological mother (Sue) had no say in how I was raised. I can't imagine how hard this must have been for her and from all accounts, she struggled on many levels with the situation.

I was aware of my family situation from a very young age and while I was incredibly loved by my adopted parents, as I began discovering the world, questions came to surface, about the situation. This lead to be-

Introduction

havioural problems and me becoming quite a rebel of a child. One thing I did notice about myself early on, was that I was super curious. I would question everything. Rarely would I look at anything and take it on face value. I also realised that "normal" was not always a good thing.

While my rebellious personality never led me to being involved in horrible crimes, I became involved with a group of mates who used to do graffiti, which led to stealing spray cans to create our artwork. We also engaged in general vandalism and small-time shop lifting, along with illegal riding of motor bikes on the highway etc. I'd say the worst thing I was ever involved in was when we would steal dad's gun powder, his fishing sinkers and copper piping, which we used to make bombs to blow up people's letter boxes. Looking back now, I am surprised I didn't die in the process; let alone end up in jail at the age of fourteen.

Speaking of jail, I did end up being sentenced to six months imprisonment later in life, but only ended up in prison for ten days. Thankfully my sentence was overturned upon appeal and hence why I was only inside for ten days. It was for sending offensive text messages, which sounds crazy that I ended up in jail for it, but I got a bad judge on a day he was very cranky, so thankfully, the legal system corrected this injustice so I could continue with my life.

The reason why I mention this, is firstly because I don't want you thinking that I am any different to anyone else facing challenges in life, but secondly, because this was a real turning point in my life. The ten days I spent in jail, tested everything that I had learn about personal development up until that moment and it forced me to dig deep into my inner strength, to find answers about how to turn that situation around and how I had come to be in that position.

We are all faced with challenges in life and sometimes we feel that life isn't fair, but I have learnt that diamonds are created under extreme pressure, so next time you are facing a challenge, remember; something special is coming. One of the best quotes I have ever read is "It is always darkest before the dawn". This is my biggest inspiration whenever times are challenging and I feel that there is no way out.

CREATE THE LIFE YOU WANT

One of my first challenges in life, was when my father kicked me out of home six weeks after I graduated high school; at age seventeen. Dad didn't do it to be a bastard, in fact, I know that he did it for all the right reasons; as strange as that may sound. At the time, I was bumming around and doing nothing after school finished. I had a casual job as a grill cook at a family restaurant, working ten hours per week, but other than that, I was going out clubbing and doing nothing. I wasn't paying board, I was constantly asking him for money and I really wasn't going anywhere fast.

At the time he kicked me out, I was pretty pissed off with him and thought that he was heartless for kicking me out of home, but pretty quickly, I learnt that he was in fact, teaching me a valuable lesson. I learnt very quickly, how to look after myself and be resourceful. There was a little bit of stealing money from unlocked cars and eating at supermarkets without paying for the food, but for the most part, I found my feet pretty quickly.

The point of me mentioning all of this, is to set you up for success by making sure that you don't think that me, or anyone else who has been successful in life, did it the easy way. I'd go so far as to say, that without the challenges, myself and the before mentioned successful people went through, perhaps none of us would have been anything extraordinary at all.

Most people, myself included up until recently, go through life thinking that life is out to get us, or that life is happening to us and not for us. We believe that our destiny is set in stone and that life is not meant to be easy. I'm here to tell you that life is however you make it. As I've learnt from almost every teacher that I've had in life, the only meaning something has in life, is the meaning that we attach to it. Everything that we experience in life, is neither bad or good. It's whatever the label we attach to the event, that becomes our reality, so this is the first key to changing your life.

Change the Way You See the World, and the World Changes

Tony Robbins has a short two-minute promotional video on YouTube, that he used to advertise his 2016 "Date with destiny" event, which got my attention. I didn't see this video until after I attended the event that year,

Introduction

but I was captivated by his words when I saw it; especially given what I experienced during the event.

The video explains exactly the type of mindset that I want you to embrace throughout this book and for the rest of your life. The first time I watched this video, I got tingling sensations down my spine and tears began welling up in my eyes, as this was the point when my whole perception of life, (past, present and future) began to change.

I loved the video so much that I transcribed his words into a notepad on my phone, so I could read it at any time. I have copied this transcript below, along with a link to the video for you to watch, before continuing with this book. Please take the time to have a quick look at this video.

If you don't want to type in the link below, simply go to YouTube and search "Date with Destiny 2016 – An introduction"

Date with Destiny 2016 – An introduction - https://youtu.be/iQztlxAUpck

WHAT IF?

What if.....
What if problems were always gifts?
What if every single problem, really was a gift in your life?
What if every problem you ever had, was life happening FOR you; not to you?
What if everything in our lives is guided?
What if everything in our lives, was divine timing?
Everything ... Even the pain!
When you're in the darkest place.
When you feel like all is lost.
When you think there is no way to turn it around.
Remember this ..... VICTORY IS NEAR!!! - Tony Robbins

To me, this perfectly explains why some people struggle through life, while others seemingly breeze through, despite everything that they experience. I know myself, that when I look back at the things I have been through, I am so thankful for them, because without those moments in my life, I would not be the man I am now, nor would I have a passion for everything that I experience in life.

Some people see the things that they experience in life, as something that drags them down, or makes them bitter, while others see the same experience, as something that lifts them up and makes them a better person. It is all in the meaning that you give that particular event, as to how it affects your life.

So, with that in your mind, let's take everything you've experienced in life, along with everything I have learnt and let's kickstart your life, beyond your wildest dreams.

Chapter One

Attitude

"It is your attitude, more than your aptitude, that will determine your altitude."
—Zig Ziglar

I briefly touched on attitude in the introduction and preface, but I think that this is the most important part of all human growth and personal development. Without the correct attitude, everything else will seem insurmountable in your quest for a better life. You may get yourself motivated to do something, but without the right attitude, that will fade out quickly. Speaking of being motivated, it was Dr John Demartini who said, that motivation is doing something you have to do, while inspiration is something that you want to do.

I remember teachers saying to me that I had an "attitude problem" at school. I never took much notice of this, because I believed I didn't have a problem with my attitude; only they did. As it turns out, my "attitude problem" was merely me understanding that I did not have to confirm to their misguided rules, that society had forced children to comply with. I now realise, that the education system in most countries, are failing to teach children the skills, that they need in the real world.

John Lennon was once quoted as having been asked a question in school as part of a project, which was; "What do you want to be when you grow up", to which John simply wrote, "Happy". The teacher turned to John and said "boy, I don't think you understand the assignment", to which John simply replied, "No, you don't understand life."

CREATE THE LIFE YOU WANT

Now, whether this is a true account, or simply a fable, it is a perfect example of how most people misunderstand the true meaning of life and all what we can achieve from it. Happiness is a state of mind and not something that can be manufactured. There are many people, who present a "fake happy" persona, when they are trying to win us over.

I'm not going to bullshit you in this book, with a bunch of sales pitches expressing "How I got ripped in ten days", or "How I made a million dollars in a year". That's how fake income scams and diet fad books work; but not me. I'm not perfect. I'm not the richest man in the world, or the fittest, but I have spent enough time studying these factors and I've seen how they have changed my life.

Many authors, spend the first chapter of their book, telling their readers, all about their qualifications, business achievements and why they are qualified to be telling you what you should do. This book, is not about me; it's about you. I have learnt so much from studying the masters of personal development, and from reading so many books, that I simply felt compelled to share the awesome information, that I have learnt, with anyone who cares to listen.

I do share stories of my own life, throughout the book, but only to bring context, to what I am sharing and so that you know that not only, do these things work, but that I am just like you. This in itself, will hopefully inspire you, to create the life that you want.

Just like you, my life is a work in progress and while I have taken huge steps to creating the life I want, I am by no means done. I have been fortunate to experience some incredible things in my life, which I have used to my advantage. I am sure that you too, have experienced similar things. Have you used them to your advantage; or seen them as a burden?

When I was in high school, I was playing rugby league and had made it onto the first-grade team. I was not your typical football player. I was the captain of the cricket team, but was a huge fan of footy. I also realised that football players got more girls than crickets, so I thought that it would be a good idea to play. I got picked to play at hooker and at the time I was

Attitude

still growing, so I was only 5 feet, 2 inches tall and only weighed sixty kilograms.

I was pretty much the smallest guy on the team. What made this fact even more obvious, was that at the time, we had two front rowers, who were the same size as fully-grown men playing professional rugby league. These two, were the prop forwards, that I had to pack into scrums with, so I was well protected.

"Big Ed" & "Big Birsy" as they were known, were both six feet, four inches tall and both weighed over 120kg each. I mean, these guys were massive. Ed, in particular, spent every single lunch in the gym and I'm not exaggerating when I say, that he was bigger than Arnie. Ed couldn't even put his arms by his side properly, because his latissimus dorsi muscles were too big.

This was great when we played other schools, because they were the biggest players on the field, but when it came to training, it was a different story. We were very fortunate at the time, that our coach, who was the deputy principle, had in fact been an assistant to Wayne Bennet, who was the coach of the Brisbane Broncos national rugby league team. Glenn, (our coach), was known around school, as being very strict. He was very tough, but in my opinion, very fair. If you were in his team, you almost got away with more than other students, because he was like a father figure to his players, so we all had a lot of respect for him.

One day during practise, we were doing drills and as part of it, I had to run at Big Ed & Big Birsy who were holding soft tackling pads. They were standing a metre apart, and as I ran towards them, they had to close the gap and make it hard for me to push through. My objective, was to run hard at them and try to bust through them, simulating busting through the opposition's defensive line, in a match.

I stood about ten metres away from them and started running towards them. As I got close, they closed the gap and pushed towards me, as I ran into them. Due to the massive imbalance in kilograms travelling in opposite directions; I came off second best. I abruptly fell backwards and landed fairly on my arse. Our coach walked over to me as I lay on the ground, grabbed me by my collar and picked me up off the grass.

I looked at Glen, as he seemed to ponder what had just happened. He said to me, "Do you know why you got smashed then?" to which I replied, "Yeah, coz they're twice my size sir." He looked at me with that fatherly look and rebutted, "No. You got smashed, because you went into it, half-heartedly." He continued, "If you had have given it everything you had, I'm pretty sure you would have made it through."

He then pointed to the starting spot, suggesting that I give it another try. I walked back to my mark, as Ed & Birsy prepared themselves. I looked at them, then glanced at the coach, to which he simply said, "Don't hold back." With that, I focussed on the behemoths in front of me, as I braced myself for another arse-whopping. I took off and ran at them with every ounce of energy I had. As I approached Ed & Birsy, I closed my eyes and prayed (not quite, but I felt like I needed a miracle). In one moment, I hit them and somehow broke through to the other side.

I stopped, turned and looked at the boys and looked towards Glen. He just nodded and smiled. I paused for a moment, smiled at my accomplishment and thought to myself, "Have I just learnt one of the biggest lessons, I will ever learn in life?" In hindsight, I now know that this was the case.

I can give a thousand examples of myself and other people, who have gone into something, or even into life as a whole and only given it half a try. We don't always commit 100%, but then wonder why it didn't work out the way we wanted it to.

The underlying lesson that I took away from that experience with Ed & Birsy, was that if you go into something half-arsed, you are certain to end up on your arse, or in pain. On the other hand, if you give it your all and don't hold back, you may still end up on your arse, but there is every chance that you might just succeed too. One thing is for sure, if you do "fail," then you will learn a valuable lesson that can be used in the future. These sentiments, have echoed through all of the biographies that I have read by successful people.

For forty years, I had a best mate named John. We met at age three, on

Attitude

our very first day of kindergarten and we instantly hit it off. We went right through school together and well into adult life, before parting ways in recent years. Throughout the book, I will refer to John, because over forty years of friendship, there were many lessons that I learnt from him. Our friendship and the lessons that I subsequently learnt, are a classic example of how life is always working *for* us.

I want to be very clear. John is an incredible man, a very kind human being and a great bloke. However, with all of John's admirable characteristics, John possesses some, not so great characteristics, that in my opinion, have held him back in life. These characteristics don't make him a bad person, but they do hamper him, in succeeding. I am not suggesting that he is anything, but a great guy. I do however, want to use these character traits, as an example, throughout the book.

John is a very intelligent man and well educated. He obtained his law degree at Bond University in Australia, which is considered one of the best universities in the world. He is a hard worker and comes from a hard-working family. The problem John has though, is that while he has incredible knowledge and aptitude, he lets himself down terribly with his attitude.

John's father, Graham, worked hard and had become a successful businessman over many years. Graham and John's mother Christine, had very little money when they met, but they sacrificed a lot, to build the future that they built for themselves and their three children; of which John was the eldest. The problem was, that this seemingly innocent mindset of lack, or that life was meant to be tough, had rubbed off on John and I don't think he ever worked out how to shake it off.

John is very close with his father, so anytime John looked to break these "shackles", his father would "bring him back to earth" so to speak. Graham meant well, but as a result of his own beliefs, Graham (in my opinion), was holding his son back. As a result of this, any discussions John and I had about how I believed he could move beyond his scarcity in all areas of his life, were abruptly met with pessimism.

I, on the other hand was brought up believing that I could achieve anything. Of course, as life went on, I was met with circumstances, that led me to believe that maybe I shouldn't be so much of a dreamer. These in part, came from John, as a result, of his own limiting beliefs. For many years, I thought that his "realistic" attitude, was a good counter balance, for my "dreamer" attitude, however the more I studied personal development, the more I realised that John's pessimism was not good for me, or himself.

I began to realise this, the more I compared how my life was unfolding, in comparison to his as we were in our thirties. While John was a great lawyer, had a wife and two gorgeous daughters, there seemed to be so much unhappiness and dis-ease in his life. He would often refer to anything that didn't go his way as "Smithy's Law". This was a reference to "Murphy's Law", where anything that can go wrong; usually does. Hi surname is Smith, so this was his thing and it was why he believed the world was conspiring to make his life hard.

I remember reading one of my very first books on personal development, which was called "You can do it" by an Australian author by the name of Paul Hanna. In the book, I read a line about someone who used to wake up every single day and proclaim, "Nothing is going to happen today, that I can't handle." At the time, I was dealing with a bitter breakup, with the mother of my daughter, who in my opinion was a complete nutcase. I was twenty-three, an unexpected brand-new father and I had her trying to manipulate me any way possible.

Looking back now, this situation wasn't the worst thing in the world, but at the time, it felt like my world was caving in. In hindsight, this situation was teaching me to grow a backbone; which I did. The quote that I read from Paul's book, was perfectly timed and I decided right then, that this would be my new mantra. I decided that from the next morning on, I would wake up and say to myself, "Nothing is going to happen today, that I can't handle." The interesting thing, was that each night, I would go to bed and think, "Hmm, nothing has happened today, that I didn't handle."

After a few months of this, I really began to understand the magnitude of this affirmation. If something did happen during the day, that I thought was impossible to handle, this quote would instantly come into my mind and I would remember that over the past month, nothing had happened that I had not handled.

So far as John was concerned though, he would wake up each morning and almost expect the day to be tough. I'm sure he didn't intentionally do this to himself, as no one would, but subconsciously, he was so focussed on what might go wrong, that inevitably, these things showed up as he expected.

One of the biggest things that I have learnt, and something that I have read in almost every single personal development book that I have read, is that what you focus on, becomes your reality. It seems like common sense, but often might appear to us to be bullshit, but if you do nothing else from this book, remember this. You will always attract what you think about most; even if you don't want it. As they said in movie; *The Secret*: "Thoughts become things."

If you look back at all the things that you now have in your life, along with the things that may not have wanted, I am certain that you will recall them being a prominent thought, at some stage, before they appeared in your reality. This was what John was creating in his life. He and his family never had enough money, despite him earning a six-figure income at one stage. He and his family were sick at least twice every year. John himself, suffered from sleep apnoea and chronic disc inflation in his back and most things in their lives, seemed to be a constant struggle.

When I began understanding the way our minds worked, I began monitoring how I was thinking and adjusting my thoughts accordingly, in order to not focus on the things that I didn't want. As I did this, I also noticed that in contrast, John was almost always focussing on negative things. Illness, too many bills etc. These negative thoughts were then manifesting in his life.

Because he was my best friend, I only wanted good things for him, so I began sharing with him, my new-found knowledge and how I was applying them to my life. This was met with his trade mark negativity and denial that this could result in any change in his life. The problem with

John wasn't so much in his unwillingness to change things, it was in his closed mind, so far as accepting a new approach.

John's grandfather, was very "old-school" when it came to doctors and psychology and this of course, was passed down to John's father and eventually John. As much as they are all amazing men, in my opinion, this was their Achilles heel.

They were of the belief, that anything that isn't mainstream, can't be true, so me bringing a new way to look at things, was quickly shot down by John and his limiting beliefs. The more I pushed this "option", the more John dug his heals in and proclaimed that he was simply meant to live the way he lived and no amount of positive thinking will ever change that.

John did attend one seminar with me, by Christopher Howard for three days, which I believe he enjoyed. However, a few weeks after the event, John was again of the belief, that all of these types of seminars, were rubbish and what he called "stuff I already know." He thought that because he already knew these things, then why hadn't his life changed, prior to these events. I did try to explain to him, that it was perhaps his outlook that was affecting his outcome, however he felt that he simply wasn't a believer when it came to people being able to change their lives.

As is the case with anything in life, "whether we believe we can, or we can't; we are correct." - Henry Ford. Over the following few years, I watched John put on more weight, get unhealthier, become poorer financially and basically resign himself to an "average" life, despite him having the same opportunities as anyone else. I on the other hand, was not about to settle for the life that I had experienced up until that moment. I was determined to find the answers that I was looking for.

I didn't have the life I truly wanted at that stage and I too questioned why I wasn't achieving the ultimate life, despite having attended seminars and having read books on how to create a better life. What I didn't realise then (but do now), was that even though my attitude was pretty good, being around someone who I thought the world of and who I trusted completely, but who was so negative, was actually affecting my own beliefs in a negative way.

Attitude

A few years passed and for reasons that are somewhat baffling, John and I parted ways. At the time, I was upset that my righthand man and best mate of almost forty years, was no longer there when I needed him. As time passed, I realised the blessing that this was. I don't mean that I would not want John in my life, but I think that if he was, it would only be if he had similar attitude towards life, as mine.

I will always respect John and will always wish him success and happiness in every area of his life, but once I was removed from that situation and the negative influence, I felt like I could become anything I wanted. I no longer had someone telling me that I couldn't completely remodel my life, or create the life that I had always dreamed of.

As I looked back at the preceding ten years or so of our friendship, I realised that I had been happy travelling the world as a professional singer. I had written books, explored over four-hundred destinations and was on the journey that I wanted. I had not been sick in five or six years and while I wasn't married (which I wanted), I was generally happy about life.

In contrast, when I looked at John's life, he was broke, his marriage was on the rocks, he was constantly sick and he believed that life was out to get him. I want you to understand that the purpose for me telling you this story, is simply to illustrate the power of our thoughts and our attitude. While John was focussing on what was wrong, he was attracting it. On the other hand, I was focussing on what was good and subsequently, I was, for the most part, attracting that.

Our attitude is the most important key to achieving a successful life. With the right attitude, we can create anything. If our attitude is right, everything else will flow from it. As Tony Robbins says, "What is wrong is always available; but so is what is right." We will always find something bad to see, if that is what we're looking for, but if we choose to look for the good, it will show up too.

Have you ever been running late driving to work? The last thing you want, are red lights. You duck and weave through traffic to get to work on time, praying that you don't get red lights. Despite this, you end up getting what you don't want. Because this is your focus, every single light turns red and slows you down.

As Tony Robbin's promo video for Date with Destiny 2016 suggested, wouldn't life be awesome if we could see where life was happening *for* us; not *to* us? Every day, things happen that ultimately guide us towards our destiny. All we need to do, is look at these events in a different way and discover how they are helping us; not hindering us.

For example; A few years ago, I was living in a beautiful hi-rise apartment, right in the heart of the sunny Gold Coast, with an incredible view over the water and a bachelor lifestyle, that most people would envy. I started dating a girl and after a short while, we moved in together. Somehow, she managed to talk me into moving into a house, way out in the suburbs, miles from work and pretty much everything.

A few weeks later, a friend was wanting someone to adopt his two pure bred Labrador dogs that he bred and sold to a couple, who could no longer keep them. My girlfriend and I agreed to adopt the dogs, but at the last minute, the original owners decided to keep them. This left us a little disappointed, as we had our hearts set on having the dogs in our lives, so within a few weeks, I bought a gorgeous eight-week old red kelpie puppy and brought him home for my girlfriend, as her birthday present.

This was all well and good, but less than two months later, she left both me and the dog, leaving me with four months left on our lease, along with all the bills that came with it. Thankfully, she agreed to pay rent for the remainder of the lease, while I purchased the $5000 worth of brand new furniture off her, that we had jointly bought for our new home.

Because it was just my puppy named Bailey and me now, I thought that least one of us should have a girlfriend, so Bailey and I went off to the local animal shelter and adopted a beautiful female kelpie, who was a month older than Bailey. Bailey, Bella (the rescue dog) and I began our lives together, but as time went on, I began thinking that maybe I had made a big mistake by taking on the responsibility of having two dogs, bills for furniture, a new lease (after we moved to a cheaper house on our own) at the same time as I was moving on emotionally.

Attitude

During the course of the next six months, I ended up being wrongly imprisoned (which I mentioned earlier) and subsequently, publicly shamed as well. There was a horrible vendetta and public smear campaign, that was being waged against me by, some ill-infirmed people, with very little morals or ethics. As this dilemma unfolded, one by one, I began losing friends, as they began showing their true colours.

Regardless, I suddenly found myself, unemployed, publicly shamed, broke from spirally legal bills, and gradually friendless. Throughout this ordeal, I did my best to stay positive and push forward, but with every day, it seemed that another hurdle was placed in front of me, at the same time as I lost more friends.

The thing that I noticed most of all though, was that no matter what happened, what people said, or even what I did, my dogs always looked at me with love in their eyes and their usual playful attitude. They couldn't care less if I had robbed a bank or had gone on a rampage with a gun. All they cared about, was that I came home to them and that I adored them.

My two dogs would always be happy to see me, want to run around and play and inevitably, whenever I was feeling down, they would make me laugh, by being completely stupid. It wasn't long before I realised, that the universe had pushed my life in precisely the direction that it needed to be, so that I was provided with the security and love that I needed at that time. Sure, it would have been nice to have a bit more human support, but there is nothing better than the unconditional love of a beautiful dog. In fact, the only thing better than the love of a dog, is the love of two dogs.

In hindsight, having very little human support, forced me to become a much stronger person, to the point where I don't need to rely on anyone these days. If I am completely honest though, looking back, without these two mutts making me laugh and providing me with a reason to put one foot in front another and overcome the challenges that I was facing, I may not be here today.

Not only did my dogs provide me with love and companionship, when no one else did, they also taught me how to be ok with being on my own and how to be at peace in my own company. This is something that just a year earlier, would have been impossible for me and led to me jumping from one relationship to another in quick succession.

I suddenly felt very comfortable within myself and with my company. So much so, that when I am in a relationship, I can give myself to that woman, without losing myself, like most of us do and like I used to do when in a relationship. The entire situation that led me to being in this house, with my dogs etc. happened in precisely the way it needed to, so that I could grow and achieve the things that I needed to achieve. While this may seem like an insignificant occurrence, I can tell you, that I now look at every event in life that I may feel is unfair or not good and realise that it is life happening *for* me; not *to* me.

This all comes down to attitude. In every situation, we can choose to fight it, hate it and deny it, or we can open our minds to the possibly, that it is helping us to reach our goals. Sometimes you may not work it out straight away, but it always shows you how, at some stage. Start now, by adopting this attitude as you look to change, or improve your life. If you kick your toe when getting out of bed in the morning, realise that this is a sign that you need to open your fucking eyes; not that life is out to get you.

Start looking for the lessons in every situation. If something happens that you don't like, stop and think, "How is this an example of life happening *for* me; not *to* me?" Another great question to ask is, "What can I learn from this," or as Tony Robbins always says, "What else can this mean?" We often think that an event means one thing, when it really means something completely different.

Often the meaning that we give an event, is nothing more than our own perception, that we have projected onto it. For example; Ladies, have you ever had a guy walk past you and say, "you look hot today?" Depending on your mood, your attitude or how you feel about your own self-worth, this compliment could have different meanings. Yes, maybe you would prefer a guy use a more flattering compliment, like saying you look "beautiful", rather than hot, but given that some men have trouble giving genuine compliments, because of nerves when in the company of women, this might be as close as you get.

Attitude

If you're having a good day, feel good about yourself, you would more than likely accept the compliment and walk away smiling and feeling even better, because of the guys attention. If, on the other hand, you're stressed at work and are perhaps feeling like the weekend's drinks that you had, have added a few inches to your waistline, then there's a good chance, his compliment will be met with a snarl or a dirty look, along with your thinking that he is a sleazebag. This is exactly how one event, can have more than one meaning, depending on our attitude. I know that this is a silly example, but this is how we tend to project our own issues onto situations, all day; every day.

"Nothing in life has any meaning, except than the meaning we give it," is a great quote that I got from Tony Robbins at his six-day seminar; Date with Destiny in 2016. Whether the cup is half full, or half empty. Whether the rain is bad or good, or a flat tyre is a good or a bad thing, is only true, depending on what we project onto the situation.

The way to find better meanings to events and circumstances, is to ask better questions. If you ask yourself, "Why do I always get speeding tickets?" You will get the answer, "Because you're a stupid fucking lead foot." Whereas, if you ask yourself, "What is the universe trying to show me here?" You will get a response more like, "You need to slow down, so that your family can have you around."

The questions we ask, determine the results we get. Bill Gates didn't ask himself, "How can I be the richest man I the world?" He asked himself, "How can I put a computer in every home around the world?" (Which eventually led to him becoming the richest man in the world). If you want better results, ask better questions. This doesn't just apply for achieving wealth, succeeding in business, or achieving huge goals. This should be applied in everyday life and in every situation, that you encounter.

Instead of thinking that the world is out to get you, or life sucks big time, ask yourself, how this is serving you. When I was locked up for ten days, I was distraught. I was due to fly to the USA and embark on a holiday of a lifetime, the day after I was imprisoned. As I lay awake in my tiny cell of the watch house, after having been sentenced, I began asking myself a few questions. These questions, not only kept me sane, throughout the ten days in jail, but they provided me with the answers that I needed, to move forward from this traumatic event.

These questions were:

1. What else could this mean?
2. What can I learn from this?
3. What is the silver lining in this?
4. How can I grow from this?

As I fell sleep on the first night in jail, I kept asking myself these questions over and over. When I woke up the next morning and throughout the ten days in prison, I kept asking those questions over and over.

I could have asked completely different questions, like most people would, when thrust into this type of situation, like:

- Why is this happening to me?
- Why does this shit always happen to me?
- How can I get revenge for this?
- How did I deserve this?

As you can see, these two sets of questions are in stark contrast. Do you think I would have received different answers and a different outcome, based on which questions I asked?

At any moment in our lives, we have the power to determine our attitude and how we see something. Sure, there are events that you might think are impossible to see any other way than negatively, but in fact, nothing in life has any meaning, other than the meaning that we give it. Take the word "impossible", for example. Put a space between the 'm' and the 'p' and you now have "I'm Possible". It all comes down to the attitude that we cultivate in our lives.

In January 2013, I lost my beautiful girlfriend to suicide. A week after her death, I was scrolling through Facebook, when I saw that my friend Rebecca, had put up a post, about how her day was going. It was mid-morning and by this stage, she had told everyone on Facebook, that

Attitude

she had a cold, got a flat tyre on the way to drop the kids off at school and subsequently broke one of her fake nails, changing the tyre.

Rebecca was venting and telling everyone how bad she thought her life was. Having just gone through the traumatic event of losing my girlfriend to suicide, I suddenly had a very different outlook to life. I sat looking at Rebecca's post for a moment, before commenting on her post with a simple, "I'll swap lives with you right now if you like." Rebecca knew that I had just lost my partner and knew that I was by no means trying to belittle her, but that I was simply giving her a "wake up call". Rebecca then replied to my comment by saying, "Thank you for the dose of reality xxoo."

Rebecca was a driven, successful woman, happily married and all in all, well off, so my subtle message reminded her, that we always have a choice as to how we feel in life, as long as we choose to have the right attitude.

This leads me to one particular attitude, that I and most successful people, try to cultivate every single day and that is the "attitude of gratitude". This is something that I first learnt, listening to Tony Robbin's "Get the edge" CD series. If you want to buy any audio series, then this one is still one of the best. Tony has a knack of taking complex issues and breaking them down into simple to apply strategies, that anyone can use to improve their life.

In Get the edge, Tony has a CD that he calls his "Hour or Power" which he urges you to use every day. Throughout the CD, Tony walks you through various "rituals" (for want of a better word), that set you up to get the best out of each day. One of the things Tony focusses on, is gratitude. I remember the first time I listened to the CD, I thought, "I don't have anything to be grateful for. That's why I bought this fucking audio series".

Just as these thoughts rushed into my brain and I began to feel like taking the CD out of my Walkman and using it as a frisbee, (Yes, it was that long ago that I first bought it), Tony said the following words that caught my attention. "What *could* you be grateful for, if you wanted to be?" He then went on to say, "What's wrong, is always available, but so is what's right".

This forced me to stop being a "Negative Nancy" and see if I could find something to be grateful for. At first, it was small things, like the fact that I have two arms and two legs. I had a roof over my head and so on. As I began coming up with these things that I was grateful for, I noticed that they were getting better and more significant. I then thought that I was grateful for the career that I had at the time, where I was paid stupidly large amounts of money to travel around the world as a professional singer on cruise ships. I thought of the talent that I had been given and the more I thought about it, the more I realised that my life was much better than I had first thought, only a few moments earlier.

Dr John Demartini, who was one of the incredible contributors on the book and movie, "The Secret" said, "What you think about and thank about, you bring about." At first glance, this may appear all "hocus-pocus", but it really is one of the truest things that I have encountered on my journey so far. Most people have seen or read The Secret, so I am sure you understand that what you focus on, becomes your reality, but have you ever stopped and thought about whether you are grateful for something, or complaining about it?

Have you ever been driving along and saw a cyclist riding on the side of the road? Your instinct is to look in the direction of the cyclist, but what happens, when you start looking at them? You start to veer towards them; which is exactly what you don't want. It is important to always focus on what you do want, and not what you don't want, because the more you focus on it, the more it is likely to happen.

One man who is living proof of this theory is Viktor E Frankl. If you're not aware, Frankl survived the Auschwitz concentration camps, in the second world war, when so many others perished. His book, "Man's search for meaning" is an incredible insight, into how he managed to keep himself alive, when so many others perished or simply gave up hope. It was his attitude that allowed him to see beyond the horrible situation he was in for many years. This is what ultimately led to him surviving, despite the seemingly insurmountable odds. It is one of the most amazing stories every written, and one that I highly recommend.

Along with Viktor E Frankl's book, I urge you to find as many books

Attitude

or audio programs on attitude or personal development in general. With the dawn of the internet, we certainly are in the information age, whereby it has never been easier to learn and grow. It is so easy to find reputable material by world leading experts, whether it be by way of seminars, books, audio providers such as Audible, or if money is a factor, then libraries and the internet can also help.

When it comes to attitude, the saying, "It is always darkest before the dawn," which for me, perfectly sums up, how life runs in cycles. Things aren't always going to be perfect and in fact, sometimes, life can seem too hard deal with. One thing I used to love about working on as an entertainer on cruise ships, was the sunsets and sunrises. At sea, these times of the day are even more beautiful than when experienced on land.

I must admit, that as an entertainer, I hardly saw any sunrises, because the entertainment team started work late, partied even later and rarely woke up before 10am. On a couple of special occasions, when coming into special ports, like Sydney, I did get up early to see the sunrise and I wasn't disappointed.

The thing that I noticed, was that in the hour before the sun rose, everything seemed darker than was the case in the early evening, or before 3am. The thing about that moment, is that it proceeds the most beautiful time of the day. Life imitates art and it also imitates nature. If you look back through your life and take notice of the most amazing times in your life, I am certain that just before that amazing moment, was a much darker place.

It is true for sunrises, and it is true for life, that it is "Always darkest before the dawn." I know that for me personally, when I am in a dark place or facing adversity, I know that the "dawn" is about to arrive. I keep that thought in mind and it definitely helps to keep me focussed, knowing that something special is about to occur in my life.

Sometimes when things get tough, we want to pack it in and give up. You may have been trying to achieve something, without success, for so long and you really don't think you can continue. Let me tell you, one thing that I have read in almost every book on success ever written, is that the single most important factor to success is to never give up. By giving up, you are denying yourself that victory, that may be just around the corner. You may have been striving for something for weeks, months or years, but if you give up, you will never know just how close you were to success.

It could be in any area of your life, but the key is to never give up. You never know how close you are to success. I sincerely wish that my partner knew how close she was to creating the life she desired, when she committed suicide. She had faced many adversities in her life, but she was growing at such a rapid rate, at the time of her death. If only she continued for another day, maybe she would have seen the success, that she had actually achieved.

There are many cases where successful people gave it one more shot and ended up succeeding. One of the most famous cases of having the right attitude and never giving up, was the story of Colonel Harland Sanders; the man who started Kentucky Fried Chicken. Colonel Sanders now famous secret recipe was rejected 1,009 times, before he became one of the biggest franchises in the world.

How many times would you have accepted rejection, before you gave up? Just think, if Colonel Sanders gave up after 1,000 rejections, we would not be able to enjoy that recipe of eleven secret herbs and spices. Colonel Sanders never gave up, and neither should you.

Chapter Two

Decide

"Whether you think you can, or you can't; you're right."
—Henry Ford

Not long after my experience with my football coach, that I mentioned in the previous chapter, I started dating a girl, who was three years older than me. I was still in high school, but she had graduated three years earlier. Besides suddenly being elevated to legend status by my mates, for dating a smoking hot blonde who was older, my girlfriend, Nicky also had her open drivers licence. This meant that because I had my leaners license, I could drive with her in the car.

This was very cool and it meant that I had a gorgeous driving instructor, who I got to make love to as well. Nicky was so patient teaching me. I owe the fact that I aced my test when it came up, due to the many things she taught me. There was one particular lesson though, that has stuck with me, until this day.

We were driving through Surfers Paradise one afternoon, when we came up to a set of traffic lights. As we approached the lights, they turned orange. My first instinct, was to brake, then I thought that maybe I should go. I hesitated, and after initially braking, I accelerated and sped up, but by the time I got to the light, it had turned red and I ran the red light. Once Nicky started breathing again, she forced a smile, then looked me and said, "You know why that happened, don't you?" I must have had a puzzled look on my face as I continued to tightly grip the steering wheel, so she continued, "It's because you hesitated."

CREATE THE LIFE YOU WANT

She explained to me, that when you see a light turn orange, the most important thing to do, is to make a decision, as to whether you are going to stop safely, or if you are can safely make it through the intersection before the light turns red. Unbeknown to me, this was my second great lesson in life. As they say, "those who hesitate are lost." As Christopher Howard said, "Even if you get off on the wrong side of the fence, you can always jump over to the right side." If you sit still on the train tracks of life, eventually, you're going to get run over, so decide.

It was early March 2016 when I was struggling for direction in my life. I had read a few books and attended a few seminars, but I couldn't seem to find the answers that I was searching for, to obtain that every elusive "wonderful life". I sat on my back deck one afternoon and the thought came into my head, that Tony Robbins used to conduct his top-level seminar; Date with Destiny on the Gold Coast, where I live, in May each year.

I searched on google for information and sure enough, his event was coming up, in just over a month. I knew how good Tony was from listening to his audio series, but I also knew how expensive his events were. I found information about the company running his event and gave them a call. While most people pay a lot less, the price I was given, one month out from the event was $7,000 Australian Dollars.

The sales consultant was very informative and I knew that the event would be incredible, however, the cost was alarming. I had always wanted to attend Tony's event, or events like it, but I couldn't justify the outlay in my mind on previous occasions, so I never went. I understood the concept, that the greatest investment we can make, is in our own education, but it was still hard to grasp spending that much money, on a six-day event.

My father had passed away in the previous November, at which time he left me a small inheritance. When I say small, it was enough for me to buy a new car and have a little left over. That "little left over" was exactly $7,000. At that point in my life, I was unemployed as a result of the before mentioned jail sentence and due to a media vendetta. I had found it hard getting a job, as people recognised me and knew my history, when I went for interviews.

Decide

I had been surviving over the past few months on bits and pieces of casual work, but it was not enough to survive on, so for me to spend my last savings on an event like this, was a big call in my mind. I told Liam, who was the sales consultant, that I wanted to think about it and hung up the phone. I called my friend Rhema, who is a wonderful lady with whom I trust completely. I said to Rhema that I wanted her to give me a simple "Yes of No" answer to a question I had. I said, "I have $7,000 and Tony Robbins has a 6-day event in May that costs $7,000. Should I go?"

Without pausing she blurted out "Fuck yes." That was precisely the type of definitive answer I was looking for. To be honest, I was hoping she would say yes, but if she didn't, I would have acted, based on your choice. I hung up from Rhema and called Liam back straight away and gave him my credit card details, to lock in my seat. Whenever I had spent that kind of money in the past, I always had a churning feeling in my stomach, having spent so much money. In this case, it was completely different. I felt relieved and excited that I had said "fuck it" and made the decision that changed my life.

All change happens in an instant. If you want to change your body, your relationship, your happiness, or anything; the first step is to decide. While this may seem too simple to be so important, it really is key and if you can master this step, the rest will seem a lot easier. I could have sat and contemplated spending that much money and more than likely talked myself out of it, but instead, I made the decision.

The old me would have spent the money on something stupid, but this time I was determined to turn things around. The funny thing, is that prior to booking for Tony's event, I was looking at buying a quad bike, to go play on. I think we both know, which was the best choice to make. Now, less than two years, later, I can buy quite a few quad bikes, with the money I have made, as a result of attending the event.

How many times have you said to yourself; "I would like XYZ," only to over contemplate or talk yourself out of it, or worse; ignore it all together. All change starts with a decision. No excuses. Don't procrastinate and say, "I will once this happens," or "once I can do this, I'll change." That type of thought pattern will hold you back forever. Make a real decision and watch how things happen.

The Latin meaning for the word "decide" is literally to "cut off". In other words, to cut off from any other option. When you make a decision to end a relationship or start a new job, buy a car, or lose weight, you are cutting off from any other option. The next step is to take action; which we will look at in the next chapter.

For some people, coming to that point where they decide is the hard part. Quite often, we "think" about changing, but never do. The reason so many people think that making a change is so hard, is because they have not established a big enough reason why they have to change. The "why" is the first thing you need to find. Once you find the why, the how and when, usually take care of themselves.

As Tony Robbins explains, there are two reasons why we do anything in life. Everything we do in life, is to either gain pleasure or avoid pain. These two polar opposites are what drive us to make change in our life. If you're overweight, you're *why* is probably pain related. You want to make the change and lose weight, because you're tired of people looking at you funny, because of your weight, or perhaps you're sick of being teased etc.

When you decide to lose weight, you are therefore doing it to avoid pain. On the other hand, if you buy an ice-cream and get the extra cream on top, with chocolate sauce and nuts; you're making that decision to gain pleasure. If, on the other hand, you decide not to buy the ice-cream, then it's clear, that you have linked more pain (extra weight gain), to eating the ice-cream, than the pleasure of eating it. These two forces are very powerful tools to create change in your life. These are what I call "leverage".

So often in life, we are mildly unhappy with something, but we don't make a change. That is the case until we get enough leverage. To use the previous weight example, that leverage might come when you tip the scales over a certain weight, that you've never done before. It might come when your favourite shirt or dress just won't fit anymore. That pain that you feel in that moment, becomes your leverage and becomes your motivating why.

While using pain as leverage to make a change in your life is great, if

Decide

you can use pleasure, that is even better. There is a stronger force for us to be pulled towards something good, than there is to be pushed away from something bad. Using the "avoiding pain" motivation, is great to start with, but in order to maintain than momentum and not go back, the trick is to use the "gaining pleasure" as your motivator is the key.

In other words, if you want to lose a lot of weight, then you would first get "disturbed" as Tony calls it. Get yourself to a point where you're so pissed at how you feel about the weight (or any other thing you want to change), then use that as leverage as motivation to propel you towards making that change. As you progress and you lose weight, you may find that you feel better about yourself, so therefore may not have the same pain relating to how you look. This is where you use the "gaining pleasure", to keep you going.

You see the results you have already achieved and you visualize yourself having lost all the weight you want and looking amazing in your new clothes. You visualize how much better your life will be when you achieve that goal and how happy you will be. This is how you use the forces of avoiding pleasure and gaining pleasure to change anything in your life. The same principle applies to any area of your life.

"When would **NOW** be a good time to start"

The above quote was one that I got from a personal development teacher from America, by the name of Christopher Howard in 2007. I remember sitting in his three-day seminar in London, when I heard this and instantly fell in love with it. I mean, it makes sense, doesn't it? "When would *now* be a good time to change?" We think about how we want to be richer, fitter, better, smarter etc, but most of the time, we don't do anything about it; other than moan about it.

Ever since I heard these words, my friends will tell you, that they will never complain about their lives to me, unless they are prepared to hear me say that quote to them. A friend will say, "I'm so fat" or "I hate my job and want to leave," to which I *always* reply, "so when would *now* (emphasising the *now*) be a good time to start?"

CREATE THE LIFE YOU WANT

The first time they hear me say it, they usually pause for a moment, tilt their head slightly to one side, like a dog looking confused and then ponder what they just heard. This is usually followed by a knowing smile and a sarcastic comment back in my direction. Either way, it always works and they always get the point.

They realise that there is no point in complaining about things, unless you're going to do something about it and the best time to do so is *now*. As Eckhart Tolle so wonderfully started in his aptly titled book "The power of now", the only time we really have is now. The past is gone, the future is not yet here, so the only moment of power we have. is in the now.

I once read (and plagiarised for my own song lyrics) "Yesterday is history, tomorrow a mystery, today is a gift; that's why it's called the present". Everything is in the "now". Things that we did yesterday, when we did them, were "now". The things we plan for tomorrow can't happen until we get to the "now", so why wouldn't you use the one power you have and make that decision right now.

During the seminar, Christopher Howard told us a story of when he and his brother were young, his parents would hide their Christmas presents in the top of the wardrobe in the weeks leading up to Christmas. When their parents were busy, the boys would grab a chair and climb into the cupboard, to see if they could guess what their presents were going to be. Once they had the present in their hands, they would hold it, shake it, smell it and feel it, to see if they could see what it was. Quite often, the only way they could really know what it was, was to somehow peel open a small part of the wrapping at one end, so they could see inside. When realising what it was, excitement filled their young minds.

The moral of this story, was that it was only when they looked inside the *present*, that they could see into the future. My point here, is that while it is good to be aware of the future and celebrate the past, it is only in the present that anything matters.

The reason I mention this is simply because now is the only moment of power we have in life. It's the only time that we can decide. You can't decide in the past, and planning on deciding in the future is just ridiculous,

Decide

because in most cases, it never happens. This is precisely why the first key to achieving whatever it is you want in your life; is to decide. Once you decide, you will find that things will start to happen.

When I say decide, I don't mean, "oh I would like to leave my partner," or "I would like more money." By deciding, I mean that you decide to "cut off" from all other possibilities. Decide and give yourself no other option, but to succeed. When you decide, you have to make it a must. Not a should, or maybe; a must.

It's amazing what the human mind can achieve when we give ourselves no other option, but to succeed. There is no point giving yourself a "maybe" or a backup plan in case you fail. That is why most people don't succeed in relationships, business, health and any other area. They dip their toe in the water, so to speak and keep one hand on the safety rail, because they fear the unknown, or they fear change.

Have you ever tried to climb to the next rung on a ladder, while still holding on to the rung below? It's impossible. You need to let go of the rung below to grab the next one as you climb higher. The same applies with moving forward in life. You need to let go of the lower rung and grab onto the next opportunity. Sure. It may be daunting or scary, but you will be surprised what happened when you give yourself no other option.

As Tony Robbins always says when he recounts how war Generals led their troops to victory, "if you want to take the island; burn the fucking boats!" Think about that for a moment. If you were faced with the prospect of either dying or succeeding, which would you choose? As Tony says, "When people have the choice to either die or succeed, they tend to succeed."

When the mind is given no way out, it will achieve things beyond comprehension. I love how Tony talks about making things a must, instead of a "should". We have all been there (me included) where we say, "I should workout," or "I should leave an abusive relationship." The problem is, until you make it a "must" you will more than likely remain the same.

Dr Wayne Dyer summed it up best when saying, if we keep saying I should this, or I should that, all we end up doing is "shoulding" all over ourselves (And what an unpleasant mess that would be). Give yourself no other option, but to succeed.

The biggest mistake most people make, is that they get in their own way, when it comes to creating the life they desire. By that I mean, that they make excuses or tell themselves stories about why they can't do something, or why their life is how it is. The truth is, that the only reason their life is the way it is, is because of the excuses they have made.

For example; I am not overweight, but I have a bit of extra fat around my waist. Let's keep it in perspective, I am pretty lean and have always been fairly healthy, but I could lose maybe two kilograms and tone up. This is not horrendous and in most people's eyes, there is nothing to be done. On occasions, I have told myself that it's not that bad, or that I just can't lose weight. Both are excuses. The truth is, that I am essentially lazy. I love eating chips and I hate going to the gym. Therefore, I have not lost those last few kilograms.

We all love to look at why our life isn't how we want it to be and justify it by making excuses. We tell ourselves that it's just how we are, its genetics or some other excuse to let ourselves off the hook. I can tell you right now, this is complete bullshit. I hate to offend anyone, but I am certain that I am about to. I am not about to apologise because it is quite simple, that if you keep making excuses, you will never achieve the results that you desire.

If you are fat, it's not because you are big boned, or anything else. It is because you're lazy, eat crap food, don't take care of your health, don't respect your body, don't exercise or a combination of these things. Stop telling yourself its ok, when it's not. I am sure you "try" to eat better and do some exercise, but if you've not lost the weight, it is because you have not made it a must, to do so. The sooner you get out of your own way and stop making excuses, the sooner you will achieve the results you want.

If you're poor, it's not your family's fault, your education, your enemies or the government. You're poor because you have a horrible relationship with money. You are not doing yourself any favours by lying to yourself in these situations. The good news, is that you can change any area of your life, by telling better stories.

Decide

Instead of blaming others or circumstances, for your health or financial situation, start telling yourself that you are healthy and wealthy (Even if you don't look it right now). You can master your life, but first you must master the stories you tell yourself about why you are the way you are.

As they say, "A problem well stated, is a problem half solved." Identify the problem. See it as it is and own it. Don't make it worse than it is. See it exactly as it is, then see it as being better than it is in your mind and make it better than it is. Once you have identified the problem, then you can work out how to fix it. Denying it, or making excuses for it, will never make it better. When you accept your shortcomings, you can improve them.

Michael Jordan didn't make excuses growing up, when he was an average basketball player. He looked at the areas of his game that were not so good and he worked on them, until he became the greatest player the game has ever seen. If you want to achieve anything in life, you have to get rid of the excuses that you are telling yourself, as to why you've not achieved them yet.

Let's take my situation, where I am not as healthy as I would like. If I deny it. More than likely, I will either remain the same, or continue to put on weight. So, what I would do is, identify the issue (being overweight and unhealthy), I see it as it is (a few kilograms and a tad out of shape) then I see it as being better than it is.

So, first I accept that I am not as fit as I would like to be. I don't put it aside, or pretend It's not there. I identify that I am reasonably healthy and not morbidly obese. I then visualize myself as a healthy and fit person, who no longer has the excess kilos. I identify why I am not losing the weight I want (by eating crap snacks) and I change that behaviour, by looking for alternative snacks to eat. I also decide to find a way to exercise, where I don't have to go to a gym. For me, this is regularly walking my dogs and being active at the beach, to burn excess calories.

If we see our problems as worse than they are, we will just end up giving up before we even start. We tend to exaggerate things when assessing our self. We either make it worse than it is, or are in denial or pretend it's better than it is. To change something, you first need to see it exactly as it is. Then once you have done that, you map out a course to get to your goals.

The reason you must identify what your current situation is before knowing where you want to be, is because without the start and finish points, you won't have any direction as to how to get to where you want to go. It's like using google maps to drive from one place to another. If you type in where you want to go, but you are not sure where you're starting from (Let's assume that google is offline and it's not able to use satellite to determine your current location), then google maps won't be able to plot your course and guide you.

If your starting point is not accurate, then you may end up at a different destination to the one you desire. That is why establishing where you currently are, is so important. This is the case for any area of your life. Health, money, career, any area that you want to improve, requires you to map out an accurate course of where you are and where you want to be.

If you're fat, say "I am fat" and own it. If you're poor, say "I am poor". Don't beat yourself up about it, but own it and get disturbed about the fact you are this way. Once you have established where you are and where you want to be, then we go on to the next step, which is to "take action".

Chapter Three

Take Action

*"If you always do what you've always done;
you will always get what you always got."*
—Unknown

Some say that knowledge is power, but I prefer to think along the lines of Tony Robbins and Dr John Demartini, when they say that knowledge is "potential power". Having the right attitude and deciding what you want in life are not worth much, if you don't follow them up by taking action.

My former best mate John, was an aspiring journalist before he entered law. He chose law over journalism and he got the best law degree in the country. He would have been a great journalist too, if he chose that field, because he is a much better wordsmith than I could ever be. The problem though, is that John never took action.

John had part written a book on his travels with Rotary Exchange in 1992 and from all accounts, it would be a great read; if he finished writing it. When I was about to publish my first book in 2011, John became inspired to get his own book finished. With his skills, he managed to find out more information about publishing and gain industry contacts, than I did and it looked as though he would beat me to the punch, when it came to having a book published. As time went on though, I kept ploughing along, doing what I could. I was inspired and determined to do what I had said I would do, whereas John, had failed to continually act on his dream.

My taking action, led me to finishing my book and publishing it, later that year, but John's lack of taking action, meant that seven years later, he still hasn't finished his book, while this book, will be my forth. John had all the talent and he was brilliant at writing, but that knowledge he had, amounted to nothing, without action. I used to take my resumes and application letters for jobs to John, so he could help me write them better. I learnt so much from seeing how he wrote. It's just a shame that that talent was let down by a lack of action. Having an idea or a desire is great, but unless it is backed up by consistent action, then you may as well not have a dream at all.

In order to take action, that leads to results, you need to have a plan. There is no point just taking any action; although this is better than doing nothing at all. There are five basic steps to ensuring that the action that you take is most effective.

The five steps are:

- Set goals
- Visualise
- Take action
- Assess & Adjust
- Never give up

Let's look at each one of these, in more detail.

Goals:

Most people know the importance of goal setting. Most of those people, also get sick and tired of authors and coaches, banging on about how important goals are. Unfortunately, most of those people, have yet to find the success that they desire, as a result of not taking care of this basic task.

If you think about what you want; it is just a dream, but if you write it down and look at it regularly, it becomes a goal. Like many, I used to have goals, but they were all in my head. I never wrote them down and subsequently, most of them never came true. It is so important that goals are written down and looked at on a regular basis. This brings into play your reticular activating system (R.A.S), which then goes about finding people, things and events, that will help to make your goals become reality.

If you just think of your goals, more than likely, you will forget them. It is presumed that you won't act on them either, which defeats the purpose of having a goal in the first place. I have my goals written in the notepad app on my phone, so wherever I go, I can look at them. I might be standing in a line somewhere, or sitting having a coffee. Wherever I am, I can have a look at them. This helps to remind me of what I want to achieve and if I've not taken action recently, it reminds me to pull my finger out and do something about it.

There was once a study conducted to find out, what the difference between millionaires and billionaires was. While there were a few minor factors, that determined the increase in wealth, the most significant factor, was the simple fact of how they approached goals. Both millionaires and billionaires had goals and both groups had their goals written down. The only difference, was that millionaires read their goals once every single day, but billionaires read their goals twice, every single day. It was this extra focus, that kept them on track and ensured that they were constantly moving towards their goals.

There are many methods of setting goals that I have learnt, but the one that I prefer is the one that Christopher Howard taught, when he was conducting his seminars a few years ago. Tony Robbins teaches a very similar structure to goal setting as well, so I have a mix of both methods, when I set my goals.

Christopher Howard called it the C.R.E.A.T.E your outcome criteria, which is as follows:

1. **CONCISE & CLEAR:** Keep your goal sharp and not too wordy. Your goal will be more affective, the more concise it is. State exactly what it is that you want, but don't overcomplicate it.
2. **REALISTIC:** Keep your goal realistic so you believe that it is possible to achieve that goal. While it's great to have a BHAG (Big Hair Audacious Goal), you want to make sure that your

goals are realistic, otherwise, you may subconsciously not think it is possible to achieve.

3. **EMOTION:** Make sure that you have emotion attached to your goal. How will you feel when you achieve that goal? This will become a major driving factor for you.
4. **AS IF NOW (Present tense):** By stating your goal in the present tense, you will be able to step into that moment and feel the feelings you will get, when you achieve your goal. This will bring extra power and emotions, which will assist in driving you towards that goal.
5. **TIMED / TOWARDS THE POSITIVE:** Make sure that you have a specific date that you want the goal to be obtained. You also want to make sure that your goal is positive and not negative.
6. **EVIDENCE PROCEDURE:** How will you know that you have achieved this goal? Add how you will know, when you have reached your goal.

So now, let's look at an example and break it down. Let's say that your goal is the following:

"It is now, January 1st, 2020 and I am smiling uncontrollably, as I drive out of the dealership, with the top down in my brand-new Porsche, that I have bought."

If we look at this goal, we can see that it is clear and concise. It is realistic (depending on your situation). There is an emotional trigger of how you will feel (I am smiling uncontrollably). It is stated as if now (It is now). We have put a time on it (January 1st, 2020) and we have a trigger for knowing when we have achieved this goal (as I drive out of the dealership).

This is the basic structure that you can use in setting every single goal. Whether it be financial like this one, or something more spiritual or emotional, it is the same formula.

Here's another example for you:

Take Action

"It is now, December 14, 2019 and I am feeling extremely proud as step onto the scales and see that I have reached my goal weight of 60 kilograms".

Notice how there is a definite emotion and evidence of this goal being achieved. This is important, so you know when you reach your goal, otherwise, you won't know when it's reached and be able to celebrate your achievement.

This leads me to an important point. Setting goals and achieving them, is great, but make sure that you celebrate each goal, no matter how big or small. You must reward yourself and celebrate your achievements. It is for this reason, that I believe that it is important to have different sized goals.

Having huge goals (BHAGs) is awesome, but they may take a while to achieve. To keep your spirits up, while chasing your huge goals, it is important to set smaller, more achievable goals. This keeps your momentum going while you're chipping away at the bigger goals. On other side of the coin, make sure that you push yourself, by setting some goals that are harder to achieve.

I like to set small and medium goals, as well as bigger goals and also a few BHAGs. The BHAGs are goals that I have absolutely no idea of how to obtain them. This forces me to step outside my comfort zone and stretch beyond my usual capabilities.

As an example, when I attended Christopher Howard's seminar, I did the above goal setting procedure with 5,000 other people. At the time, I was writing my first feature length screen play. My goal was to receive a "best screenplay award" at the Academy Awards. Now, this goal is still ongoing as I am still writing it, so I'm yet to fulfil this goal. After we set the goal, Chris took as through a strategic visioning process, where we stepped inside that goal and visualised it being achieved.

Once we completed that process, Chris asked us all to come up with a goal that we had absolutely no idea how we were going to attain it. I thought for a minute and decided that I wanted to receive a "Second best screen play award". I turned to my mate and shared this goal with him.

He knew that I was working on the first screen play, but as far as he knew, I didn't have an idea for a second screen play.

He said, "You don't have a second screen play to win a second award with"? I nodded my head and said, "I know". A month later, while working on the first screen play, I came up with a brilliant idea for a second screen play and a year later, I had written the second screen play. FYI: The second screen play is a sequel to the first one, so it can't be released until the first one is made.

My point here is, that by setting the huge goal that I had no idea how to achieve, it set off a series of events and thoughts, that led to it being manifested, where it didn't previously exist. This is why it's important to set all types of goals; both big and small.

Visualise:

Once you have your goals, the next step is to see yourself achieving those goals. The incredible thing about the mind, is that it can't tell the difference between what is real and what we vividly imagine. The body can achieve anything that the mind can conceive. For years, we have known that all things that we have created in our world, first started out as a thought and a feeling.

The key to bringing things from your internal world, to your external world, is to see them as already being real. This is done through "visualisation." Visualisation, is where you get an exact imagine of what you want to achieve in your mind and see it and feel it as if it has already become reality. At first this can be a little tricky, but with practise, anyone can do it.

There was an experiment conducted back in the 1990's with a college basketball team, that proved this theory to be true. The students were broken up into three groups. Each group was asked to shoot hoops. Their scores were calculated and averaged out among their induvial group.

Following this, the groups were each given different instructions. The first group was told to come back in three weeks, but were asked not to do any practise between now and then. The second group was told to practise

Take Action

shooting hoops for twenty minutes every day, for three weeks. The third group were told to *visualise* practising shooting for twenty minutes, every day, for three weeks.

The three groups returned as instructed, three weeks later. Each group were once again asked to shoot a series of shots. The first group shot almost the same as their previous attempt, three weeks earlier. The second group that physically practised shooting hoops, had an improvement of 20% from their previous attempt. The third group, despite having had no physical practise for three weeks, had a 60% improvement.

The reason why the third group improved so much, was because they visualised shooting hoops. They visualised getting the ball in the hoop over and over until their mind knew exactly how to do it successfully. When it came time for them to do it for real, their body simply followed the instructions that the mind gave them, which led to successfully shooting more hoops than the other groups.

The mind is an incredible thing, and visualisation, brings the body into alignment with the mind, so that we can achieve whatever we can vividly imagine. From my own experience on stage, I would always visualise myself performing a song or routine perfectly on stage, while I was in rehearsals. As a result of this process, I only screwed up on stage on one or two occasions.

Once you have your goal clearly written, then close your eyes and put yourself right inside that goal. If you have music that you want to use to help you, then that is great, or perhaps you might like to meditate on that goal. Whatever works for you is fine. The most important thing, is that you see, feel and hear the sounds, sights and feelings that are associated with that goal, so it becomes real for you.

I have Christopher Howard's strategic visioning process from his seminar, so I use that to embed the goal into my subconscious mind. I usually only do it once, then I turn it over to the universe, to start the manifestation process. If you want, you can visualise your goal over and over, to really get it into your subconscious.

Take Action:

Once you have completed the first two steps, then it's time to take action. There is no point, having great goals, if you do nothing about them. Probably the most important action that you take towards your goal, is the one you take immediately after setting the goal. Far too often, people set goals and that is it. They create beautiful goals, but do nothing about them.

As Tony Robbins says, "Never leave the site of setting a goal, without doing something towards it's attainment." Use the power and emotion of the moment, to do something. If your goal is to lose weight, then it could be as small as calling a few gyms, to get prices on memberships. It doesn't have to be the biggest of actions, just make sure that you do something to achieve that goal, right away.

You will be surprised how this gives you momentum and the more momentum you get, the faster you will achieve your goals. Taking action is critical to achieving your goals. Without taking action, they are merely dreams. If you are consistently taking action, there is a higher chance, that you will achieve your goals. Your initial action, doesn't have to be huge, it just has to happen. Make sure that you do things as often as possible, towards your goal.

Assess & Adjust:

If for some reason, you've set your goals, visualised them, taken action and for some reason, you're not achieving your goal, then it might be time to assess the goal, or adjust the action that you are taking. As Albert Einstein said, "The definition of insanity is doing the same thing over and over, and expecting a different result."

Sometimes, even the best laid plans, need to be re-evaluated. I am presuming that you haven't set a goal and expected it to happen the next day. Goals can take time, so it is important that you don't just give up on it, if it hasn't happened as fast as you had liked. It may be that you set an unrealistic time frame for it to happen. If though, you have been taking

Take Action

consistent action and after a long period of time, nothing is happening, then it might be time to adjust your approach.

One of the biggest road blocks people face in reaching their goals, is when their goals are not aligned with their values. I've met dozens of people who say (for example), that they want to be wealthy, but don't know why, after so long, they aren't wealthy. The thing that I too didn't realise until recently, was that unless I aligned my goals with my values, then there was very little chance, that I would achieve the goals.

If someone has a goal to be wealthy, but their number one value is significance, then there is a good chance that spending money to look good and to be popular, is more important than creating wealth. If someone has a goal to be extremely fit, but their highest value is "security", then there's a good chance that they will get more security from a large block of chocolate or a packet or chips, than they will, from getting off the couch and exercising regularly.

I am of course, pointing out some pretty obvious examples of where people's values don't match their goals, but the fact remains, that if you're values and your goals are not in alignment, then there's a good chance that this is the reason, that you're not achieving your goals in that area of your life.

Having goals for the sake of having them, is a sure-fire way to never reach them. Unless your goals are aligned with your values, then you will more than likely not pursue them beyond a few days, or weeks. When I completed Date with destiny, with Tony, I discovered that my number value was "growth and learning", so when I set myself the goal of reading one-hundred books in a year, I smashed it out of the park and ended up reading more than two-hundred in the year.

If you're not achieving your goals, a simple adjustment to the action you take, can make a world of difference. You might be working out to lose weight, but the fat just won't budge. It might be as simple as the type of exercise that you are doing. Change it up and try different things, until you find what gets results.

Never Give Up:

If there is one thing that is above all else, when it comes to succeeding in life; it is never giving up. There are thousands of success stories, about how people were so close to giving up, when they gave it one last push and ended up achieving their goals. I was told in high school that I would never be a good singer, by my teacher. Thankfully, I didn't listen to her, or the countless others who said, that I would not be a professional singer, without formal training.

If you never give up; you can never fail.

There was a true story of long distance swimmer, Florence Chadwick, who was the first female swimmer to swim the English Channel; in both directions. Florence wanted to be the first woman to swim the twenty-one miles from the California Coast, to Catalina Island.

On the day of her swim, the water was bitterly cold and the weather was not nice. The seas were rough and there was a heavy fog in the area. The tides and currents were also against her for the swim. Despite the conditions, Florence decided to attempt the swim.

Several hours into the swim, Florence said to her coach, in the support boat, that she was too tired to continue. The conditions had gotten the better of her and she didn't feel she could go on. Her coach told her that even though she felt tired, her stroke was still really good, so Florence decided to continue.

Fifteen hours into the swim, Florence once again stopped and told her coach that she was too exhausted to continue. Her coach lifted her into the support boat and just as the support boat headed for land, the fog lifted and there was Catalina Island only half a mile away. Florence said to her coach, "If I could have seen it, I would have kept going."

Sometimes you may not be able to see how close you are to your goals, because of the fog in front of you. Sometimes, all you need is a little faith and to be able to see through the fog, so that you don't give up. If you give up, you will never know just how close you are to your goal. No matter

Take Action

how hard it is, if you keep your eyes on the goal and keep going, you will eventually get there.

So far as Florence was concerned, she tried again two months later, and despite the fog being just as dense, she kept going. Florence completed the swim in 13 hours and 47 minutes, breaking a twenty-seven-year-old record and becoming the first female to complete the swim.

Something that Dr John Demartini constantly says, when talking about goals, values and being happy in life, is that you must do what you love and love what you do. In his words, "When your vacation, becomes your vocation, then you are living a truly inspired life." It is no mistake that people like Dr Demartini and Richard Branson, work fourteen-hour days, seven days a week. They love what they do. When you're inspired to do something, you have so much more energy and resilience. I can tell you firsthand, that when I wanted to become a professional singer, I would spend hours every day, carefully going over every single note in a song, so that I was able to perform that song better than anyone else in an audition.

I spent hours and hours fine tuning my voice and learning everything there was to learn. That is what led me to being so highly paid and so blessed to be able to travel the world for ten years, doing what I loved. Success has little to do with talent, and almost everything to do with persistence and dedication. The thing that enables that type of dedication, is having the right values to match your goals. When you have them in alignment, there is nothing that will stop you from reaching your goals.

"Do what you love and you will never have to work a day in your life", is a quote by Confucius, that typifies my point here. One man who did exactly that was Hugh Hefner. He did exactly what he loved and whether you agree with his lifestyle or not, he never "worked" a day in his life. His life was one big party. It was just yesterday that Hugh Hefner passed away, so it is fitting that he has the final word on the chapter on taking action. He was famously quoted as saying, "Life is too short to be living someone else's dream."

Chapter Four

Learning & Growth

"The best investment you will ever make is in your own self-education."

—Jim Rohn

Think about this for a moment. If you were to read for just one hour a day, seven days a week, for a year, that would be the equivalent of nine times forty-hour working weeks, that you had dedicated to a subject (or subjects). Imagine what you could learn, or master, with that amount of time spent in one or more areas of your life. We are all given the same amount of time each day, but those who achieve greatness, use their allocation of time, more wisely than most.

Most people spend a high proportion of time on Facebook, or watching cat videos on YouTube. If they are not doing that, then there is a good chance, that they are watching an endless amount of TV. While there is nothing wrong with doing any of these things (if that is what you choose to do), if you want to achieve something meaningful in life, then you may want to try a different approach.

If instead, you dedicated one hour of that time to reading, or listening to an audio book, I promise you, you will excel in that subject very quickly. People like Tony Robbins, Warren Buffett and Bill Gates, dedicate a minimum of 2-3 hours every day to learning, or expanding their minds.

Learning & Growth

If you think you don't have the time, don't worry. I will share my secret to achieving this, in a moment.

The reason why I recommend reading over social media or TV, is simply because both TV and social media are making you dumber, while reading, will make you more intelligent and more grounded. TV is full of advertisements. These ads are often, misleading. Social media is full of self-absorbed narcissists, who portray their life as being mind-blowing, when in reality, it is mind-blowingly bad. Social media breeds self-esteem issues, along with other social diseases.

Most people watch TV, advertisements and social media and think that all, most, or even some of what is published is real; it's far from it. Do yourself a favour and limit your time on these platforms. If you must spend time there, don't be gullible with the content that they provide. My advice, is to question everything you see and hear. This should be the case in most things in life. Question things, instead of taking it all as gospel.

When it comes to learning, not all formats were created equal. While books nourish the soul, the media (news programs, magazines and papers), are the bottom feeders of the chain and hold no nourishment for you, or your mind. It's kind of like the difference between a professional massage and a "happy ending" massage. One is good for you and while the other may feel good at the time, afterwards, you are left feeling poorer and seriously violated.

Journalists too, are merely prostitutes in suits, selling their souls for a quick fix at the expense of anyone who's not afraid of catching what they've got. The media organisations they work for, are the pimps, with the flash cars and homes, controlling their slaves, who know no better, than to be brain-washed to the cause. Much like prostitutes, most journalists think that they are doing society a service, but don't actually realise the "dis-ease" they are infecting us with.

- Note: I really don't have an issue with prostitutes. I am simply making a point.

Let's face it, the media are not reputable in any way. They are not paid to tell the truth. They are paid to attract attention. Just like the little girl crying wolf, or Chicken Little saying that the sky is falling, the media are needy and insecure. They are needy like an insecure child who cries for attention and a cuddle. But unlike the innocent child, the media are anything but innocent. The media are more like parasites, who prey on the ignorant.

Why do I dislike the media? Well this wasn't always the case, I grew up believing that the media were informative and an important part of society. In some small way, the media are still important, but only when it comes to being notified of events that may affect our safety, such as earthquakes and flooding. Even these events are overexaggerated by media outlets though.

Unfortunately, the necessity for these types of events is rare. For the most part, the media distort the truth, to attract viewers and subsequently, advertisers; which pay their bills. They don't care about who they hurt or offend in the process and have no one to truly regulate their behaviour. They are a law unto themselves.

The age of the Internet has bred a swarm of bloggers and commentators who only survive as a result of clicks on their pages. This has meant that them and the media need to continually up the stakes, when it comes to attention catching headlines and stories. They cannot survive without page traffic that brings them advertisers, so the only way they can grab our attention is to shock us more each time.

This has led to so many cases of fake news, misleading news and downright ridiculous stories. All of this is not overly bad for me personally, because I know the truth about the media and choose to ignore it or laugh at it.

The problem is, that this type of behaviour by the media, fuels huge amounts of anger and abuse by the public. It leads to unwarranted abuse, violence and crimes such as stalking, harassment and defamation via social media, that was fuelled by the media or bloggers. The public read the misleading stories and get so uptight and upset, that they begin to lash out at each other. This creates systemic anger and leads to violent relationships and even suicide.

Why am I am telling you this? Because, while I want you to nourish your mind with empowering material. I want to forewarn you, that a lot of what is circulating, is utter rubbish. I am sure that you have a "bullshit radar" and can detect fake news, but for those who may struggle in this area, I want you to be aware of what you are feeding your mind.

Just like a plant, the right food for our brains, can make a huge difference of how we grow. One of the best descriptions about growing that I've ever heard, was when Tony Robbins talked about how everything needed to grow. He explained that everything in life is put on the earth to grow. Throughout its life, it continues to grow, until it begins to die; then it becomes fertiliser for other things to grow.

This is so true and even more so for humans. If we're not growing, then we're dying. In order to live, we must continue to grow. We don't have to grow as a rate of knots, but we must build at least a little, every day. To grow muscles, we must work out and to grow our minds, we must learn. Most of us finish school, or in some cases college or university and that's it. We think we've learnt all there is in life.

Our minds are just like plants, which need food to grow. The interesting thing is that once we start to learn, we realize, that there is so much growth to achieve. As Albert Einstein said, "The more I learn, the more I realise how little I know and the more I realise how little I know; the more I want to learn."

Become a Student of Learning

When I left high school, I had no desire to go to university or college. My opinion was that I had just endured twelve years of classes and teachers, so the last thing I wanted to do, was to pay to put myself through more torture. I left school with reasonable grades; Ok, so there were rubbish grades. I put that down to the fact that I was too busy playing cricket, football, being the lead in the school musical (Grease), performing in Rock Eisteddfod, going on snow camp, school camp, music camp, geography camp and generally doing anything *but* school work, so it was no wonder that my grades sucked.

CREATE THE LIFE YOU WANT

Throughout school, I found myself questioning everything. I was not one to confirm, or accept things on face value, like most kids. Children grow up questioning everything. They ask questions, explore everything and don't just accept things as adults do. Unfortunately, as they grow up, this is figuratively beaten out of them by way of society and school. They lose their curiosity and inquisitive natures, until they become "good little robots".

I too fell into this category and as adult life pigeon holed me into a "normal" kind of life, I thankfully discovered that this was not how life was meant to be. As I stated in the previous chapter on deciding, change happens in an instant and it was pretty much one instant, or in fact, one statement by Christopher Howard during his three-day seminar that changed everything for me.

It wasn't a grand statement and I'm sure the comment washed over several attendees, but it was when he said, "Be a student of learning," that my consciousness changed. He said that if you commit to becoming a student of learning, you will find learnings in the most bizarre places.

I must digress slightly for a moment, to tell a story of this. Christopher Howard, said this statement on the final day or his three-day seminar "Breakthrough to success." I had attended the seminar in 2006 in Brisbane, but this time, I was in London attending the event in 2007 when the statement really hit home.

In my opinion, Chris was a great teacher and I enjoyed his seminar so much, that I had to go back, only a year after the first time. Chris has set us up on the very first day, through a series of processes to prepare us for the following two days. Chris loved to tell stories and on day one, he was telling the audience a story of how he travels a lot and how when he travels, he has his favourite carryon baggage, which he takes everywhere.

While telling the story, Chris was walking around the audience of five thousand people, carrying a small suitcase. As he told the story of how he is always the last on the plane, and had to climb over people to get to his seat, he was literally climbing over the audience, carrying his baggage. As he did so, he explained that no matter how long his journey was, or

Learning & Growth

how old or irrelevant his baggage was, he would still take it with him everywhere he went.

The audience was amused by Chris' story and as he stepped back up on stage, he placed his suitcase at the back of the stage and moved onto a different topic. I remember thinking to myself at the time, that it was a little strange, but I let the thought go and enjoyed the rest of the seminar.

Fast forward to the final hour of the final day. Over the course of the three days, we had done so much work on removing limiting beliefs, letting go of our pasts, visualising the future and preparing ourselves for the next chapter of our lives. Then it all fell into place. After three twelve-hour days, I had learnt so much, but I felt like there were some loose ends in my mind. I turned to my friend Anita (who was there with me) and said to her, "It all hinges on this last hour, as to whether this guy is good or great."

This is when Chris emphasised that he wanted us to become students of learning. He said, "If you commit to becoming a student of learning, you will find learnings in the most bizarre places; like on airplanes." The lights in the room then dimmed slightly and Chris turned a high stool around and sat backwards on it, facing the audience and continued, "And as the plane touched down and everyone stood up and began reaching for the overhead lockers, the captain came over the intercom and said – **LEAVE YOUR BAGGAGE HERE.**"

An almost silent, but slightly audible collective sigh from the audience, filled the room. We all got it. We all understood at a deeper level, that the past does not equal the future. We do not need to go through life carrying baggage, that doesn't serve us in any way. The thing that really hit home for me in particular, was that when I was ten years old, my teacher told me that I would never be a good reader. She obviously saw me struggling with reading and for some reason thought that she would plant that idea in my young mind, instead of encouraging me to be better.

With that limiting belief firmly planted in my head, I hardly read at all for the next twenty years. I only read one book in school and read a couple of self-help books around the age of twenty-five, but other than that, I believed that I was never going to be a good reader.

CREATE THE LIFE YOU WANT

Fast forward to 2017 and as of today, I have read over 300 books on personal development. Over 280 of these have been in the last fifteen months since attending Tony Robbins' seminar in 2016. I have become the "student of learning" that Christopher Howard had suggested and I recommend that you do too.

Like many things in life, I used to make up excuses about why I didn't read. Besides the fact that I was told that I would not be a good reader, I used to say to myself that I don't have the money or resources to buy books, or the time to read them. As Chris Howard, Tony Robbins and many others have said, "It is never a case of resources, only a case of resourcefulness". If you want anything in life, it is never a case of resources (Money, time etc), it is always a case of how resourceful you are.

As fate would have it, I started looking at audio programs at the library after attending Tony's seminar when I discovered the greatest resource I had found this far. Because I had not set foot inside a library in twenty years, I had to sign up for a library card. The lovely assistant explained to me that on top of the hundreds of thousands of books that the libraries throughout my city had, they also had a new app called "overdrive" which had over 50,000 eBooks and audio books that I could borrow.

At first, I thought nothing of this information, but when I got home and began searching, I discovered that there were over thousands of audio books on all the topics that I was interested in. Everything from money, investing, health, spirituality, you name it, this app had it. I had found the geeks version or heaven.

A moment ago, I hinted at how I managed to read so many books in a year, so this next part is my gift to you. I don't care how busy your life is, or how much you think you don't have time to read, you too can plough through as many books as I have, using the same method. I'm very lucky that the Gold Coast City Council Library system is the biggest in Australia, because it is two councils that merged over ten years ago, as the Gold Coast grew. We are very blessed, but I am certain that wherever you are in the world, that you have similar opportunities as I do through your local library system.

Learning & Growth

What I suggest, is to get down to your local library and sign up, then ask them if they have a similar app and how to use it. Ask them if they are linked to other libraries in your city (which they most likely will be), or even other cities around the country. I often borrow audio from one library and return it to another (while searching for a new title there).

Here's the good bit. Once you have found eBooks or audio books, you will be able to read fifteen to thirty hours per week, regardless of your schedule. Here's the kicker though; you must not make excuses. You must commit to finding the time, I am about to explain, that we all have available to us.

We all have 2-3 hours per day, that we can use to listen to an audio book. "Yeah right", I hear you say. It's true. Here's how. Let's say that you drive to work for thirty minutes each day, to and from work. That's one hour, times five days a week, that you could be listening to an audio book. Why listen to advertisements on the radio or mindless talking, when you could be expanding your mind, listening to a topic that you're passionate about. That topic might be about how to create that killer body, that your partner will adore. If you're single, then it might be on attracting the right partner, or it could be an audio book on making a million dollars. It's your one hour, so you choose what you are learning.

Do you watch the news, or TV when you get home from work? If so, then there's one to four hours each night, that you could be reading an audio book too. I'm not suggesting that you become as obsessed with reading as I did, but if there is an area of your life that you want to improve, then this is the easiest way to learn how to do it.

I put my headphones in and listen to an audio book while cooking dinner. I appreciate that not everyone has that luxury, because of family commitments. Connection with family is extremely important, but I'm certain that there is some time each day, that you can find to listen to an audio book.

The news is so misleading and negatively slanted, that it is creating so much depression in the world, so why not mute it and empower yourself instead. Using this time to read, is what I call N.E.T time or No, Extra,

CREATE THE LIFE YOU WANT

Time. It's so simple, yet so effective. We tend to go through life wasting time throughout the day. I'm not suggesting that you don't relax or watch TV. All I am saying, is to be mindful of where you could use this resource and use your time more wisely. The one thing we all have that is the same, is time, so why not make time work for you.

I personally love listening to books on my way to work or driving around town. The app is downloaded on your phone, so you can listen anywhere you want. I listen while driving, walking on the beach, while making dinner at night, while walking my dogs, in bed before going to sleep and anywhere I am doing something that I can do so.

So many people complain about their life and wonder why it sux, but if they looked at how much time they waste watching mindless TV, it would be clear. Don't bitch about your life. Get of your arse and do something about it. My former best mate was a classic example. He would spend four hours a night and eight hours a day on weekends, in front of the TV, but he was puzzled why he was 40kg overweight and so unhappy in his life.

If you're watching TV all the time or spending hours on social media, then I will bet you're not happy with your life and more than likely dumbfounded as to why this is the case. Social media and the news are the source of so many problems in the world. Everything from terrorism and illness are cause by the media's constant misdirected influences and constant focus. In my opinion, if you want to get rid of something, the worst thing you can do is focus on it, so it's no wonder people are getting sicker and terrorism is becoming more influential when the media are constantly fuelling both.

As soon as I realised how detrimental to my happiness the media was, my life improved out of sight. I urge you to take everything you see, read or hear in the media, with a grain of salt and a large dose of scepticism. If you do, I promise you that you will be much happier.

Instead of damaging your mind with media rubbish, read a book or listen to an audiobook, then watch how much better you feel in a short amount of time. Another great resource that you can access using NET time, are podcasts and YouTube (but not for cat videos). There are so many great podcasts, on every topic imaginable and there are literally hundreds of thousands of YouTube videos on personal development topics. Tony Robbins, Warren Buffett, Jim Rohn and many more, have stacks of videos of their seminars online for free.

If I find myself unable to find a good audiobook for a week or so, I go looking for podcasts or YouTube videos on topics that I want to learn about. There are endless free resources available to all of us, so there are no excuses.

If you want some cutting-edge programs to sink your teeth into and are willing to make a small investment in yourself, then there are plenty of good ones available to buy.

Tony Robbins has various audio programs on his website www.tonyrobbins.com ranging from personal development, wealth, health and many more. Tony also has online courses available at very reasonable prices.

Dr John Demartini has online courses, DVD's and audio courses on his website www.drdemartini.com as well.

With the accessibility of the internet these days, there are so many programs you can buy, but if money is a factor, then please consider your local library, because I am sure you will be surprised with what they offer these days. Libraries also buy their books, based on recommendations from the public, so if you want a particular book, let them know.

Be Like a Child

It is my belief that one of the keys to creating an incredible life, is to become "insatiably curious" like a child. Look at the world like you're looking through a child's eyes and ask questions of everything that you see and encounter. Asking questions will lead to answers and this will lead to a greater understanding of everything around you, as well as yourself.

If you want to become great at anything, you need to ask questions, but if you want to master a subject; then you need to become obsessed. When

CREATE THE LIFE YOU WANT

I look back at the areas of my life that I was extremely successful at, it was no coincidence that they were the areas, that I was obsessed with.

Being obsessed, saw me go from a wannabe rapper, chasing a record deal, to become one of the most highly decorated lead male vocalists on cruise ships anywhere in the world. It was only through my obsession with practising every single note, and scrutinising every aspect of my performance, that allowed me to choose whichever cruise ship, or contract that I wanted, while many performers were struggling just to get a gig.

I then used that same obsession to learn everything there was to learn about cruise ships, to the point where Australia's second largest law firm tracked me down, so I could provide expert advice for court cases pertaining to cruise ships. Now, I am obsessed with learning more about myself and sharing that knowledge, so that others can benefit from it.

If you want to achieve greatness, you must become obsessed with learning your craft in that area of expertise. It can be your career, health or anything you desire, but if you want better than average results, then you must become better than average, when it comes to learning.

It was Jim Rohn who said, "If you work hard on your job, you can make a living, but if you work hard on yourself; you can make a fortune." In this quote, Jim was referring to self-education. While I am of the belief that the education system worldwide needs a dramatic overhaul, there are still some great things that children are taught at school. For those who are wondering who Jim Rohn is, Jim was hugely successful personal development speaker and the man who taught Tony Robbins everything he knew in his early days. Tony attended one of Jim's seminars and ended up working for him.

Most great leaders in the world also believe that the education system is failing our children. They all agree that change must happen, but this is a long way away, so self-education is pivotal in your success in life. My older girlfriend (Nicky), that I had in grade twelve, said to me that I would learn more in the first three years after school, than I did during the twelve years at school; and she was right.

I have learnt so much, just by living in the real world that school didn't teach me, so it made sense that it was up to me, to make sure that I educate myself too. The thing about the formal education system as it stands now, is that most children are not engaged in the learning process because of the content that is being taught. It is no coincidence that children are being told they are suffering from ADHD and Autism. It's not the children who are the problem, it is the way the children are being engaged by an outdated system.

Therefore, I strongly recommend self-education throughout life. Find what you are passionate about, then find all the available resources you can find, to become a master of that topic. This is precisely what I did with finance. I stumbled across finance and discovered that I enjoyed it, so I again become obsessed and began learning as much as I could on the topic.

As a result, I am now formally qualified in finance, while also being educated at a much deeper level, because I chose to self-educate myself, rather than having it pushed onto me. If we are passionate about something, we are much more likely to absorb the information and learn faster. At school, we were taught certain aspects of finance but none that I have used to date. Who has used Pythagoras theorem or algebra since high school? I haven't and I'm sure I'm not the only one. There are so many examples of wasted curriculum in schools, so why not find what you do want to learn about and go out and learn all about it.

Dr John Demartini often says, "When your vocation becomes your vacation, then you're living a truly inspired life." If you find what you truly love to do and do it every single day, then it won't feel like work; it will feel like a holiday. Have you ever noticed that when you're doing something that you truly love, time seems to go so fast, but if you're doing a job that you hate, the days seems to last forever?

This happens when you're either passionate, or not passionate about what you're doing. This is where learning can help. If you find something that you're passionate about, then you will feel compelled to learn all about it. It goes without saying, that all you need to do, is find where your passion lies and then learn all there is to learn about it. If you do that, then there is no doubt that before too long, that thing will be providing you with a sizable income, even though it seems like you're constantly on holiday, because you're doing what you love.

Richard Branson was asked how he never has a day off, to which he replied, "because I never work." He doesn't see what he does as work; he sees it all as play. He has meetings, buys things, builds things, creates companies and it's all play to him. That is why he can work fourteen-hour days, all year and not get burnt out.

The greatest achievers in life all work endless hours, but it's what they love doing, so it's never a struggle. The one thing that they all confess to though, is that to start with, they were all obsessed with learning and obsessed with succeeding in what they were doing. This book may be your first, on your journey, or it may be your one-hundredth. Either way, this is the beginning, or a continuation; never the end of your learning journey.

Chapter Five

Wealth

"A gold medal is a wonderful thing, but if you're not enough without it, you will never be enough with it."

—John Candy in *Cool Runnings*

This chapter on wealth, will be by far the longest and most in-depth chapter in this book. This is because, this is the subject that I am most qualified in and the one that most people either neglect, or fail miserably in. Wealth is also the area, that if mastered, can create an incredible springboard for you to build your wildest dreams on.

So often in life, we desire something, that we feel will make us happy, or change our lives. The reality is, that when we reach that goal, often, it not only fails to achieve the feelings we had hoped it would, but in many cases, it leaves us even more unfulfilled. John Candy's character in the movie *Cool Runnings* summed this up perfectly. Candy said to his lead sledder, (as the young athlete appears solely focussed on how winning a gold medal will make him happy), "A gold medal is a wonderful thing, but if you're not enough without it; you will never be enough with it."

Candy's point, was that he wanted to make sure, that his team were striving for their goals for the right reasons. The same is true for money. Money is a wonderful thing. It can allow us to create the life we desire, but if we are chasing money for the wrong reasons, then there is every likelihood, that it will disappear from our lives, even faster than it arrived.

We strive for a better body, better relationship, more toys and more money, thinking that these things will miraculously be the cure for our emptiness in some area of our life. Of all our desires and goals, I think money is the one where this is most obvious. While money can't buy you happiness (according to some people), it can buy you a jet ski and having owned jet ski myself, I've yet to see someone unhappy, while riding a jet ski. I am of course being sarcastic, but in a way, it's kind of true on both accounts.

My ex-girlfriend (The one who committed suicide), said to me, that she wanted to get breast implants, so that she could feel better. I personally thought there was nothing wrong with her breasts, but I understood her reasoning for wanting them bigger. I did have a concern though, that the underlying issues that led her to feeling inadequate without large breasts, were more important to address, rather than the actual size of her breasts.

By this, I mean that while I'm sure she would feel more "womanly" and therefore confident if she was able to fill out bras and swimwear, I honestly believed that this would be only a temporary fix and not resolve the issues that may have led to her feeling this way in the first place. In her case, I was of the belief that she would still have the same issues, but with bigger breasts.

This seems to be the case for many women on the Gold Coast where I live. Per capita, The Gold Coast would probably have more women with breast implants, than anywhere else in the world; other than maybe Hollywood. Literally, every second woman walking down the street, has implants. I am not suggesting that this is a bad thing, but, for the most part, these women appear to be very insecure, so it makes me wonder what their motivation was.

How does this relate to a chapter on money? Well, the feeling we have about a lack of money, or our issues surrounding money, will not go away, by simply having more money. Sure, money can buy you a bigger house, better clothes, a flashier car and so on, but once the euphoria of these things wears off, more often than not, we are left wanting more and in most cases, end up with more debt and even more money issues, than we had when we were broke.

Most lotto winners are completely broke and in debt within a few years

Wealth

of their windfall and there are as many cases of suicide among the wealthy, as there is with the poor. This has to be proof that money alone, cannot buy happiness. Money can, assist in launching your greatest desires and enable you to follow your dreams.

I wanted to make this point at the beginning of this chapter, so that you can remember this, as you strive for greater wealth. Both financial wealth, as well as spiritual wealth. When I attended Tony Robbins' six-day "Date with Destiny" seminar, Tony was teaching the audience about what he called the "Science of achievement" and the "Art of fulfilment". Tony went into great detail teaching us about how there is a science to achieving success and how there is an art to being fulfilled and how if we have one without the other, then we will not be truly happy.

I won't try to emulate this here, as it is far more complex than I could do justice, plus, I'm not about plagiarizing anyone's work, but I will tell you this. Tony told us a great story about everyone's favourite comedian; Robin Williams and how despite having conquered the world in every endeavour that Robin wanted to, he was still not fulfilled. This lack of fulfillment, led to his eventual suicide. How can a man who is adored by millions of people around the world and who has reached the pinnacle of success do this? Quite simply, he mastered the science of achievement, but he was unable to master the art of fulfilment.

By now, I think you will realise that I am not just wanting to provide you with tools to improve your life. I really want to ensure that you have a foundation that will become the solid base, that you build all of your dreams and achievements on. The reason for this, is because I too once had tools, but had no foundation to hold them all together, when I went after them. It was like building a building on soft sand. I'd set off chasing goals, with all the gusto in the world, only to run out of steam when I was constantly building and destroying my own goals.

Ok, by now you're thinking "come on dude, get to the fricking point and give me some tools so I can make some money". Ok, let's get started.

One thing that I've learnt as a result of the nearly one-hundred books that I have read on money, investing and finance, is that there are some

CREATE THE LIFE YOU WANT

fairly simple keys to accumulating wealth. Despite this, hardly anyone does them. There will be much of what you read in this chapter that you will think is "common sense". Let me tell you, while this stuff is in my opinion common sense, it isn't that common, when it comes to the number of people who actually apply it. Common sense, often doesn't lead to common practise.

If you're not wealthy, or as well off financially as you want to be, then it's simple; you have not yet fully understood these simple principles. My advice therefore, is that while you may have heard all of these key principles, until you fully get them at the cellular level, you won't get where you want to be financially.

There seems to be a casual mindset in most countries, that the government will look after you, as you run out of money. From my understanding, this could not be further from the truth. In Australia at least, the old aged pension, is less than most people need to live on. In Australia, the most a single person would receive on the pension, is $23,096 per year. That's a pathetic $444.00 per week. And for a couple, the maximum is $34,819 per year ($669.00 per week).

If you can live on that, then that's fine, but for me personally, that would barely pay my rent and feed me, let alone pay for expenses, bills, medication etc. Most workers in Australia receive superannuation from their employers, which they can access upon retirement. The problem with this, is that hardly anyone has enough superannuation to last them beyond ten years after retirement. If you think I am simply painting a bleak picture, to scare you; you're right. But that doesn't mean that what I am saying is not true.

Most Australians and from what I understand, people in most countries, do not have enough savings, or will not receive enough government benefits in retirement to survive, let alone, to enjoy life. For me personally, when I retire, that is the time that I want to live it up. I want to travel, spend money and enjoy life, not sit around broke, not eating properly and wondering how I am going to survive. This is why I did exactly what I am about to explain to you and you can too. I promise you, that if you get a

Wealth

grasp of the following pages, you will be so much better off, when it really matters; in the best years of your life.

Like most people, I have always wanted more money. I had read a few books and thought I knew what to do, yet I was still broke. It wasn't until after Tony's seminar in 2016 that a friend leant me Tony's number one best seller "Money, Master the game" as an audio book. We had a peer group from the seminar and we would meet once a month to help each other and keep each other on track after the event.

During that time, one of the women in the group, who had accumulated great wealth, asked me a question that really changed my mindset towards money. Her question was simply, "What is your relationship with money?" On first evaluation, it seemed like a basic question, but for the next few days, I began to think more deeply about it.

Over the last two years, since that question was first posed to me, I have been on a mission, to not only answer that question and improve my relationship with money, but to discover a few other questions, that are just as important, to achieve financial freedom.

I want you to take a moment and ask yourself the following questions. Take your time and answer them with complete honesty. The answers to these questions, will tell you a lot about why you may not be as wealthy as you want to be. If you're already that wealthy, then it's always a great opportunity to fine tune things and refocus.

- What is my relationship with money?
- How do I feel subconsciously about money?
- How do I spend my money?
- What is my plan for retirement?

While the answers that your provide, from the first three questions, will give you an insight into any underlying "money issues" that you may have, the last question, is the one that I really want to focus on, in this chapter. Anyone who has failed to plan for retirement, has planned to fail. Unless, you are happy being poor and living a less than average life, in retirement, then depending on the government, is not an option, so let's cross that option off, right now.

Given my own financial position at the time of my friend Aly asking the first question, it was clear that my relationship with money was shit. I had a lot of debt, no savings, no assets (other than a car and some furniture) and I was also unemployed. It was then that I started taking ownership of the situation and began looking for ways to turn it around. Less than two years later, the turnaround is flourishing, and yours can too, in just as little time; regardless of where you are financially, right now.

I want you to know this, so that you can realise that it doesn't matter where you are starting from, as long as you start. By taking ownership of your financial journey, you will be surprised at just how quickly things fall into place. I must be clear, that at no point have I earnt a huge wage, or had a high flying corporate job paying $150,000 per year. Quite the opposite. One thing that gave me hope, was that there have been many wealthy people, who have created their own wealth, while earning modest wages. This means that you can to, regardless of your situation.

Robert Kiyosaki first opened my eyes as to how this can occur, in his best-selling book, "Rich Dad, Poor Dad." In the book, Robert explained that there are four types of people, when it comes to earning money. The first two, are employees and self-employed people, who in most cases, will never be rich. The other two types, are business owners and investors, who are far more likely to become wealthy.

The reason for this, is that the first two groups of people, earn money by exchanging their time for money. This is well and good, but given that there are only twenty-four hours in every day, you are limited to how much you can earn. The second two groups though, make money work for them. The business owners have employees who work for time, while the business owners build products or services which make money for them. With this, there is no limit to how big the business can become, or how much money it can make. The investors invest their money in companies, so that it is money working for them, all day and night; even while they sleep.

In order for the first group (employees and self-employed) to become

Wealth

wealthy, they need to create a second income. For example; selling books (as an author) or selling products online or subscriptions online. This allows the person to be receiving a residual income 24-hours a day; regardless of how much you work.

My books sell on websites, such as Amazon and are available to customers around the world, so this means that 24-hours a day, people can buy my books and I receive money from them, even if I am laying on the beach. There are literally thousands of ways to create a residual income, but that is another book, in itself. I suggest researching the various opportunities of online sales, as they can be financially rewarding.

The other option for employees and self-employed, is to invest their money into businesses, or companies. By investing, you are not only earning money, by being paid for time that you work, but your money that is invested, is constantly working for you. "How do I do that?" I hear you say. I thought you'd never ask, so let's get started.

Of all the books circulating in the world about how to become financially independent, Tony Robbins' "Money, master the game," is one of the very best. It is more than six hundred pages (the paperback version) and about eighteen hours of audio in total, when listening to it. It's not a quick read, but it was this book, that launched me to a whole new level, so far as money and wealth.

The book would normally take two to three weeks to listen to, but I was so obsessed once I started, that I finished it in one week. Beyond all the wonderful wisdom that I gained from the book, the biggest thing I personally gained from it, was a new-found obsession with learning more about money. It was this obsession, that led me to reading another eighty-plus books on finance, in one year.

Most of the books that I have read on finance and in particular, investing, gave advice on what the author thought was a good way to invest, but their approach, was from a place where it was presumed that the reader already had in the vicinity of $100k to invest. This advice was fine for those in that category, with money ready to invest, but what about most people, who don't have any savings?

CREATE THE LIFE YOU WANT

I want to take the tact, of first giving you the tools to get to that place, where you will have money to invest. Then, we will look at the following steps, of how to invest it and create more wealth. As much as the advice that I read was all good, it was kind of like putting the cart before the horse, for most people. I personally, don't want to leave anyone behind. I'm presuming that, just like me a few years ago, you're starting from scratch. If you're not, then you're one step ahead of the majority.

In my recent studies, and through chatting to friends and colleagues, I found that most people don't have much financial education, or knowledge; other than earning and spending money. If, you do have a large amount of money saved already, then great. The first part of this chapter, will further solidify your strategy for wealth creation and perhaps, you will pick up a few extra strategies, along the way.

In my opinion, you can never learn too much, or have too much information. This leads me to the first principle to becoming wealthy.

Key principle number one: Take an interest in all things money.

Money would be probably the least favourite thing for most people to talk about, read about or be interested in. In fact, in many social circles, talking about money is taboo. This is why most people struggle financially. I'm not saying that you have to become an accountant or a financial advisor, like myself, but for most people, money is the subject that they put in the too hard basket, or simply don't even think about.

Many people go through life with a wing and a pray that each time they need to pay a bill, that there is enough money in their account. The main reason most people don't think about money, is because they either think it is too hard to understand, or worse, if they figure it out, they will realise how financially screwed they are. I myself was in the latter category, but after many years of financial pain, I decided that enough was enough. I used to live from pay day, to pay day and most of the time, I ran out of money before my week ran out.

As I was reading "Money, master the game," I was enjoying it so much, that when I went to see my accountant a week later to do my tax return, I asked him if he could advise a good financial planner. I began looking for someone to use as a financial planner, but after having read Tony's book, I really wasn't satisfied with anyone that I found. So, what did I do? I decided to become a financial planner myself. A slightly obsessive idea, but none the less, five months later, I had completed my Diploma of Financial Planning, as well as my Advanced Diploma of Financial Planning. I will confess, along with my obsessive personality, I also studied full-time, so I graduated in a quarter of the time, these courses usually take.

My main reason for doing this wasn't necessarily to have a career in the financial industry, but more so, that I knew what to do for myself and so that I always had control of my financial destiny. One of the biggest things that Tony talks about in his book, is that we tend to trust advisors, who we think have our best interests at heart, when really, they are more interested in their own wealth creation, than ours.

This is not to say that all financial advisors are this way, but there is a decent amount in the industry who are, so it's a good idea to know enough about money, so you are not taken for a ride. It's like a woman taking her car to be serviced and being ripped off by the mechanic, who realised the woman has no idea about cars, so he takes advantage of her. In both cases, it is important to know enough about the subject, to avoid being ripped off.

The other reason for being savvy enough, when it comes to money, is so that you can grow your knowledge, along the way. If you give your money to a professional and they lose it by making bad investments, you will be pissed off and no doubt not use them again. On top of this, you will probably not trust any other advisors, for the rest of your life. While that approach won't see you lose more money, it won't help you making more money either.

On the other hand, if you make a mistake and lose money, when you are in charge, the key difference, is that you will learn a very valuable lesson and therefore not likely make the same mistake again. This in effect, is how you will build wealth. If you take a real interest in your own financial situation and education, then you will be surprised at how fast you will accumulate wealth. We all make mistakes and I am certain that like me, you will make errors in investing, but these lessons will serve you well in the long term.

Legendary investors like Warren Buffet and Ray Dalio say that there are two rules to investing. Rule number one: don't lose money and rule number two; read rule number one. I like to take a slightly different take on this. My rule number one is still the same; don't lose money, but my second rule, is that if you do lose money, make sure you learn from it. If you make a poor judgement and lose out, take a look at what you did wrong, then work out how to not make that same mistake again. Like anything in life, mistakes equal success.

As I learnt early on, we all lose money, but the fact that I made the mistakes myself and not through trusting someone with as little knowledge as myself, meant that while losing money was a painful experience, I learnt a great lesson that will stop me from making the same mistake again.

I urge you to read as many books on finance, investing and economics as possible. There are thousands of great books, eBooks and audio books available on these topics. A great resource to buy these online iTunes (for audiobooks), you can subscribe to a service such as "Audible", or you can visit your library. I have a list of books on finance / money / investing, at the end of the book.

Now is the time to take a good look at your financial situation. Go through every aspect of your financial life and make sure that you understand what is happening. Make sure that you understand exactly where your money is coming from, where it is going and how you can make the most of it. This leads me to my second key principle to becoming wealthy.

Key principle number two: Never pay full price for anything

This key, will be the shortest, because it is the simplest. It may seem like a logical statement, but do you know the importance of implementing this attitude? I never pay full price for anything; unless it's an emergency, or just a litre of milk. I only buy clothes when they are on sale, my car is

Wealth

purchased at a well negotiated price, my electricity and phone contracts are negotiated, my groceries are bought when on special and I only buy shares in companies, when they are at a heavily discounted price.

If you simply decide that you want something, then pay whatever price is listed at the time, you are throwing away thousands of dollars every year. To some, this may seem like overkill and a time waster, but let me tell you, for the small amount of effort; the benefits can be huge. By applying this strategy just on your weekly shopping, you can literally save hundreds of dollars each year.

For example: The brand of coffee that I buy, generally retails for $10, but every 2-3 weeks, it's on special, for $6. I go through a jar once a month, so if I buy it only when it's on special, that's a saving of $48 each year. The moisturiser I buy, retails for $11, but, again, once every few weeks, it sells for $7. This gives me a saving of $48 each year.

Even items such as chips can save you money, when bought well. I buy three packets of chips, each week. I vary which type I buy, depending on which one is half price that week. This saves me $468 each year. Fruit and vegetables in particular, can fluctuate greatly in price, so adapt your shopping list, according to what is in season and you will save a few more hundred dollars every year. Just because you like strawberries, doesn't mean you should buy them when they are $6 a punnet; especially when they can get as low as $1.50. One week, broccoli might be $5 per kilogram, whereas a few weeks later, it is $2.

If you apply this theory, you will save more than one thousand dollars every year, with very little effort. The key is to keep any eye on what is on special. Supermarkets spend millions of dollars each year printing catalogues, which advertise their weekly specials. Most people throw them out, but if you take a few minutes each week reading them before going shopping, you will save so much money.

When it comes to non-perishables, always buy them on special. Even if you don't need them right away. Buy them and store them, for when you run out. If I know that I'm going to run out of coffee by next week, but coffee is on special this week, I buy it. Everyone knows this theory, but very few do it. If you're a family of four, the savings will run well into the thousands. This money can then be allocated towards savings or investments; which we will discuss shortly.

When I buy clothes, I mostly buy my clothes in the end of year, or end of financial year sales. The exact same clothes are usually 50-70% off. If I want to buy something for the house, such as a new TV, mower, or appliance, I do a little research, note down prices, then wait for them to go on sale. You would be surprised, how often everything goes on sale. All you need is a little patience.

When buying a car, it is the same. I find the car I want, find out the ticket price, then wait for it to be on sale in the end of year sales. This is when car dealers desperately need to move stock, so you can bag a bargain. I always go to several car dealerships (and make it known that I am doing so to them), then let them fight it out, for the best deal. Even then, I don't accept their ticket price. They usually kick and scream and make up stories, of how they are losing money; bullshit. Stick firm and be prepared to walk away, and they will eventually move closer to your asking price.

When it comes to buying property, this is an area, where people often let their hearts rule their head and end up paying way too much. My friend's father told me, before I purchased my first unit, several years ago. "If you don't offend them (The seller), with your first offer, then you have not gone low enough." All sellers (and car dealers), add on an amount to their price, to allow for negotiation. No matter how much you love the home, unless you have money to throw away, never pay even close to the asking price. If you miss out on that one, another one will come along and it will more than likely, be better than the one you missed out on.

Lastly, when I travel, I never pay anywhere near what most people pay for flights, cruises, hotels or anything. I don't force the travel agent to eat into their commission, by screwing them down either. I used to be an travel agent, so I know, that their livelihood depends on commission. Most people think that it is a travel agent myth / lie, when they tell you, that prices never get cheaper. While it was once true that you could get great last-minute deals (ten years ago), that is almost never the case, these days. Trust me, having worked in the travel industry, I have seen so many clients get irate, when they didn't listen to me, when I said this, then their flights (that they didn't pay for), got more expensive.

This is why I always book my flights ten months out from my travel dates. That is when they are at their cheapest. Because of the way all flights are held in the worldwide booking systems, there can only be one of each date (EG: 2 September) in the system at any one time. Therefore, flight schedules are added into the systems, around eleven months prior to travel. The airlines then put them on sale, ten months out, from the travel dates.

Cruises will almost always be at their cheapest, when the prices are first released. The cruise lines releases cabin prices somewhere around eighteen months prior to departure. This is when they are the cheapest. The only exception to this, is if cabin sales are very slow, on a particular voyage, and they want to fill cabins. Even in this case, you're still looking at twelve months prior to sailing, that this occurs, so book as soon as you can.

An example of this, is when I took a Caribbean cruise, Las Vegas trip and white Christmas, all in one holiday. With flights, the cruise, hotels, car hire, shows and insurance, because I booked as I recommended above, by the time I left, the total price had increased by over $2,500. It's a good thing I booked early. By never paying full price for anything, key principle number three, becomes that little bit easier to achieve.

Key principle number three: Spend less than you earn.

This is probably the simplest, yet least utilised principle of all. We all know that the way to wealth, is to spend less than we earn, so why don't we all do it? Quite simply, most people would rather have something now, and receive the instant gratification, than have "delayed gratification". This is the case because for most of us, it is difficult to weigh up the benefits of something that is ten, twenty or thirty years down the track, as opposed to something that we can see, feel and have right now. I concede that it is much more fun to have something now, than get excited about missing out on it, for the purpose of having something that we can't see.

The amount of debt that households are carrying these days, is staggering. Not all debt is bad though. Debt that involves paying off a house, is fine (although I do weigh this up later too). Where most people go wrong though, is by going into debt for things such as overly expensive cars, furniture, jet skis, clothes etc. Consumer debt, or credit card debt, is what destroys most people financially.

Instead of waiting until they have enough money to pay for something, they buy items, to gain immediate pleasure, but fail to consider that they have to pay it off eventually. They also fail to consider how much interest they will pay in the process. Unless you are disciplined and pay your credit card off every month, this can be the biggest burden financially. In most cases, those who are using the credit card to buy items such as televisions etc, are the ones, who let the interest accrue and get out of hand.

We've all had debt; me included. I was hugely in debt on a few occasions, but learnt the hard way, that this was not a good way to be. My first taste of the "debt lifestyle", was when I went to Los Angeles, when I was twenty years old. I took off, with nothing more than a plane ticket and $1000 limit on a credit card. During the ten days that I was in L.A, I had a sporty little hire car and a nice room at the Sheraton, near Santa Monica pier, which cost me $200 per night.

I was living the high life, enjoying all that L.A had to offer. I was six days into my trip, when reality hit. I was shopping in Rodeo Drive, looking at the coolest red, white and blue leather jacket, in the style of the star-spangled banner. It was one that singer Bobby Brown would wear and what I thought was cool at the time. The jacket cost $450, so I thought, "I'll put it on the credit card and worry about how to pay for it later." I grabbed the jacket and went to the counter to pay by credit card. When the cashier tried to put through the transaction, my card declined.

I was disappointed that I didn't have enough money on my credit card to buy the jacket, but what I didn't realise, was that I had *zero* money on my card. This was 1993 and well before credit card transactions were instantaneous. The cashier in those days would have to call through for authority, so while missing out on the jacket was disappointing, it was about to get a whole lot worse. I went back to my hotel and began to feel hungry. I looked in my wallet and saw that I only had $10 in it. I had no other money and I had four more days in L.A, until my flight home.

Long story short, a friend wired $50 over to me, which arrived a day later and I was able to eat, (When I say eat, I was living off $1 hotdogs from 7/11 stores, because that was all I could afford), but my hire car and hotel charges had not yet been added on my credit card. Back in those days, most transactions took several days to register on your credit card, so when I finally arrived home and all of the credit card transactions were added weeks later, I had racked up $10,000 in ten days.

An awesome effort, I thought, but in hindsight a really stupid move. This was not the biggest problem. I was blacklisted and had a default on my credit file for five years, which meant I could not get any sort of credit. By the time I paid the debt off, it was six years later and close to an additional $3000 in interest, on top of the $10,000, that I had to pay.

The moral of this story is, that if you don't have the money now; then don't buy it. The only time I use credit cards now, is if I know for certain that I will be able to pay the full amount off before the due date; before interested gets charged. I know I can pay the credit card off every month, because I have enough savings to cover the entire limit of the card. I really only used the card, to delay making a payment because I get an interest free period on the card. I have a basic credit card that has no annual fees and no fancy loyalty schemes.

If you want to be financially secure, the first lesson, is to live within your means. If you can't afford it, you can't afford it. Going into debt is the fastest way to financial ruin. If you're the type of person, who loves to spend, with no thought of tomorrow, start to curb your desires for things now and learn to save, so you can have them.

It is easy for us to look at a new boat, or clothes and know how good it will feel to have them now, whereas, putting money away now, without the same "euphoria", is a difficult concept for the human brain to comprehend.

CREATE THE LIFE YOU WANT

It all comes down to mindset. I too was the same, until I stumbled onto a simple exercise that changed the way I saw spending, forever.

We all get the concept, that saving rather than spending, creates wealth, but how easy is it to spend money on coffees, dinner, clothes and other items, which give us instant gratification now, rather than save money for something that we can't see or touch right way. Several authors and finance gurus have called this, the "Latte factor".

In short, this is the concept where if we were to cut back on buying one latte a day, or buying lunch one day per week or limiting our spending in small ways, it can make a massive difference to our net worth in the long run. For example; let's say that you spend $5 each day on a coffee on the way to work and $10 on lunch; instead of making it at home. That's $105 per week that you could be saving and investing. I too love my coffee and the convenience of buying lunch instead of making it, is so easy, but once I grasped this concept, I realised the power that it held. Now I make my lunch every day and rarely buy coffee.

I know this sounds very boring, but I have now realised that these very small sacrifices, are in my opinion, well worth it. It really is a matter or working out for yourself, what is more important. Is spending crazy amounts of money now and being broke in the best years of your life, when you're unable to work more important OR making a few small sacrifices now, in order to have a life where by you can spend more money than you had ever dreamed of.

A couple of things I have learnt along the way, when trying to spend less than I earnt, have been the cornerstone for my financial growth. These are simple things you can do to save money and in turn, have more to invest.

Let me be clear, I am not saying you have to be an absolute miser with money and watch every single cent, but if you just spend money like a sailor (and having been a sailor, I know how we spend), then you will end up with more "month" at the end of your money; rather than more money at the end of your month.

I want to keep things in perspective, so if you can constantly save money and still enjoy life, that is great, but if you're struggling financially, yet always living the high life, it is pretty clear where the issue is. I'll use my former best mate as an example again. He's certainly not the only person who does this, but I know firsthand how his family throw away money and how they could be so much better off financially.

Him and his wife, earn good money and like most people spend it easily. Their combined income has for the most part, been more than $110,000 per year. They have no mortgage, average rent and two daughters who are old enough to work casually after school. At a glance, it would be presumed that they would at least save something each week, yet they are close to $30,000 in debt. The debt they have is not loans on cars or flash boats. The money they owe is on credit cards and to electricity and phone providers, because they have been behind on payments for years.

It blew my mind, how this could happen. I see it all the time where families or individuals earn good, or at least reasonable wages, yet they are in so much debt. What blows my mind more, is when you see them always eating out, buying smoked salmon every week for home, constantly drinking and basically throwing money at anything they have an urge for.

Tip one: Make a budget

I am not suggesting that you have a boring life, or miss out on the nicer things in life, however, to reach your financial goals, you may have to make some sacrifices along the way. One of the easiest ways to ensure that you are not spending too much, is to have a budget. I know that this is a swear word to some people, but without a budget, how will you know how much you're spending? Oh that's right, you will know when you run out; right?

Especially these days, where we rarely use cash to pay for things, it is so easy to spend without keeping track of where your money is going. I have a very simple budget, which includes a small amount of spending money. The reason I give myself spending money is simple. If I try to stick to a strict budget, with no room to move and no "play money", then it's more likely that I'll cave in and spend even more, than I am supposed to.

It's the same as having a "cheat day" on a diet. If you restrict yourself too much, it will only lead to failure in the long run. My budget is simple. I work out how much I need for rent, shopping, petrol, bills and spending, then the rest is savings. I even have a set amount when shopping, so I don't over spend and eat into my savings. I'll explain in more detail how to formulate the budget, in a moment (in Tip 3).

Tip two: Have a grocery budget and a shopping list (And stick to both)

As I mentioned in key number two, never pay full price for anything. This is especially important, when shopping for groceries. If done right, this is the area, that never paying full price, will reach the greatest benefits.

Each week, I have a set amount of money that I am allowed to spend on groceries. This amount cannot change. Yes, occasionally I splurge, but only when I know I am not breaking my savings plan. These rare occasions may be when I get a bonus pay, or an extra amount of money from somewhere. The best thing to do with any bonuses, is to save them, but let's not be too strict, to start with.

The first thing to do, is to set a reasonable shopping budget. One that is not over the top, but not too tight either. You need to eat and eat well. There is no point living on baked beans and toast, because that will lead to illness and cost you more money in the long run. Set a realistic shopping budget, but make sure you stick to it.

When you go shopping, write out a list. Don't just walk down the aisles and grab whatever grabs your attention. What I do, is I have a notepad in my phone, called "shopping list" and as I go through the week and run out of something, or think of something I want to buy, I add that to the list. This list includes toiletries, so if you need to buy makeup, cleaning products etc, include these in your grocery budget amount.

As I shop, I keep a rough tally of what amount I am up to, as I grab things off the shelves. You don't need to count exactly, but try to keep track, so you don't blow your budget and look like an idiot if you have to put things back, when at the checkout. If I get to my budget amount and I still have one or two things on my list, I look to see if I grabbed more chips than I need, or something like that, then put it back, so I can get the most important items. If on the other hand, I get to the end of my list and have money left over, I might grab something extra, or perhaps a cleaning product I know is close to running out at home.

I hardly ever go over my budget, but if I do, it is by $1-$2. This is because I usually stock up on toiletries and costly items, when they are on sale, so I have a backup at home. I try to spread my expensive items out, so I am not buying them all in one week. For example, I might buy toilet paper one week and shaving cream, but buy washing powder the following week with dishwashing liquid. This means I am only every buying one or two expensive items each week and therefore not going over budget.

Using this plan, means that when I run out of something, I usually have a spare in the cupboard. This also means that I never have to spend more than my budget as an emergency. This may seem a little tedious at first, but it's really simple and very effective in ensuring that you never over spend on groceries and therefore eat into your savings.

Tip three: Reduce/manage your bills.

Monthly expenses such as power and phone, car insurance and other bills, kill a family budget faster than anything else. It's important that you take a few steps to bring down these costs as much as possible.

This tip, is one that hardly anyone does, but it is easy and will save you heaps of money. The first thing I did to reduce my electricity costs, was to go and buy energy saver globes, for my entire house. This cost me $25 total, for my house and I noticed a huge difference in my electricity costs in the next bill. It also saved me money, because energy saver globes last much longer than normal globes. Four years on, from replacing all of my globes, and I have not had to change one single globe yet. Normally, I would change on average, one every few months, so this exercise has paid off tenfold already.

Once I had the house running more efficiently, I started comparing providers, to get better deals. I called around to find a cheaper electricity deal, a better phone plan, cheaper car insurance, home contents insurance and boat insurance. It took me less than two hours all up and it ended up saving me over $150 per month by doing so. I didn't go to inferior providers. I just asked for a better deal, or found a cheaper – comparative product. Competition is so strong these days, that providers are willing to do anything, to gain new customers.

I do this exercise once a year, or every two years, to check that I am still getting the best deal in the market. I urge you to do the same thing and see how much you will save. Once I have all of my bills reduced, what I do is I work out how much each bill costs me, every week of the year.

The way I do this is, I firstly work out each bill on a yearly basis. I go through and find every single bill that I pay throughout the year and workout the yearly cost. If it is a phone bill which is monthly, I multiple the monthly bill by twelve to give me the yearly cost. If it is car registration which is yearly, I leave it as is. If it is an electricity bill which is quarterly, I multiple it by four.

Once I have each bill as a yearly cost, I then divide each bill by fifty-two. This gives me the amount that I need to put away each week, so I always have enough money to pay the bill, when it arrives. For example, if you have a phone bill that is $60 each month, you will multiply it by twelve, which gives you $720 total for year. Then divide $720 by 52, for the number of weeks in the year. This gives you an amount of $13.84 per week. If you get paid every fortnight, then divide the yearly total by twenty-six. You do this same calculation for all your bills. Once I have all my weekly amounts, I add them together and that is the total amount that I must put away each week to meet my commitments.

The reason I do this is so that I don't get hit with four or five bills at the same time, and have to pay them all and subsequently blow my weekly budget. For me personally, my weekly total bill cost is $145, so *every* week, when I get paid, I transfer $145 into a separate account, which is only to be used for paying bills. This account accumulates, until I receive a bill, at which time, I use the money in that account, to pay the bill. By doing this, I never have to stress about finding a big amount of money for bills,

Wealth

I never blow my weekly budget, and I always have enough money ready to pay all my bills.

What this does, is it makes sure that when I have an amount I want to save or spend each week, I still do it consistently. If you try to balance it, using different amounts every week, it becomes too hard and all falls apart and you will never save. Don't try to juggle a budget where you're paying different amounts each week. It won't work.

What do you include in your bills calculations? I include, car registration, car servicing, tyres, home or contents insurance, phone bills, boat insurance, memberships that I have to pay during a year, electricity, school fees, uniforms, council rates, dog costs (registration fees, vaccinations, tick treatment etc), or anything other than really big expenses such as a mortgage or car loan. I keep car loans or mortgages separate, because of their size.

Here's how a family budget might look using this formula.

EXPENSE	AMOUNT / WEEK
RENT / MORTGAGE	$400
FOOD	$200
BILLS (TOTAL)	$250
PETROL	$60
SPENDING	$100
SAVINGS	$200

These amounts will vary for singles, couples and each family, but it gives you an idea of how it works. I know I am really breaking things down simplistically, but I want you to understand how easy it is. Make sure that you give yourself a little left over. I try not to account for every single dollar, because if the budget is too tight, it's more likely to be thrown out.

Once you have established your budget, if you find out that you're over the amount that you earn, you're going to have to look at where you can cut costs. Using the simple comparison exercise with bill providers, will save you quite a bit. Otherwise, it might be a case of not being too spend thrift. We all want nice things, but the simple fact of the matter, is that if you can't afford it and still save, then you can't afford it. My friend and his family were always spending money on BBQ's, for dozens of people and buying lavish seafood for these events. They always ate takeaway or dined out at least once a week, but they wondered why they were so far in debt. Live inside your means; not outside of it.

There is a general rule of thumb that says that you should be saving at least 10% of your wage each week. If you have a mortgage, then you might see this as saving, but as I explain shortly, putting all of your money into your home, may be a good idea in one sense, but not necessarily the best long-term option. The best approach is if you can pay off your mortgage and also put a little aside to invest in other things, which I explain soon.

That little extra money each week, you can start to do what Robert Kiyosaki explained in his book "Rich Dad / Poor Dad", by investing in other companies.

Key principle number four: The power of compounding

Making a budget is a great start to saving money and becoming financially independent. Once you have a budget and a little extra money to put away each week, you then need to work out what to do with that money. There are many options to make your money grow. Some will grow fast, and others not so fast. As we move through the remainder of this chapter, I will explain some of these options in detail. Before I do, I want to explain something that when understood, will change your financial growth more than anything else.

Most people know, that if you put your money in a bank or invest it, the money you deposit, earns interest, or dividends. What many don't know, but what rich people do know, is that there is a wonderful thing called compounding. In many cases, people invest money and when they earn interest, they simply take the interest out and spend it. Similarly, when investors invest in shares and receive dividends, then tend to take the dividend payout and spend it.

Wealth

An important thing to note, is that while it is tempting to do this (take the money and run), if you leave the interest in the bank, or reinvest the dividends back into your shares, then compounding will grow your investment, much faster than if you took the windfall. Put simply, compounding is where the interest you earn, or the dividend you receive, is added to your initial deposit and then becomes the new amount on which the interest, or dividend is then calculated.

So, instead of you earning interest on just the deposited amount, you earn interest on the deposited amount, **plus** the interest that you earnt from the previous period. As long as you don't touch the interest earnt, this continues to grow. At first, it will seem to be growing very slowly, but as momentum builds and compounding takes full effect, your savings will suddenly explode of the chart.

I want to take you through a very simple exercise that I did for myself, that blew my mind. I was looking at my budget, (that we just discussed), when I was curious as to what the outcome would be, if I was to not spend $100 per week and instead save it, or invested it. The moment I did this exercise, is when I got the "ah-ha, this is what is possible by not buying that coffee" moment.

Tony Robbins gives a fantastic example of compounding in day four of his audio series "Get the Edge", which is on finance. He talks about two friends playing golf who decide to bet ten cents per hole, compounding for each of the eighteen holes. For this example, let's say we're betting $1 per hole, compounding.

At first glance, this may not seem like a big bet, but if the amount doubles on each hole, it turns out to be a huge bet and you had better be a good golfer, if you're committing to this bet. For example, hole number one is worth $1, hole two doubles to $2, hole three doubles to $4. As the table below shows, by hole number nine, you're up to $256 and that's just the beginning.

| HOLE 1 | $1 | HOLE 10 | $512 |
| HOLE 2 | $2 | HOLE 11 | $1,024 |

CREATE THE LIFE YOU WANT

HOLE 3	$4	HOLE 12	$2,048
HOLE 4	$8	HOLE 13	$4,096
HOLE 5	$16	HOLE 14	$8,192
HOLE 6	$32	HOLE 15	$16,384
HOLE 7	$64	HOLE 16	$32,768
HOLE 8	$128	HOLE 17	$65,536
HOLE 9	$256	HOLE 18	$131,072

By hole number eighteen, the bet that was originally $1, has become an unbelievable $131,072, simply from the power of compounding. The thing about compounding, is that while at first, it appears to be growing slower than grass, once it starts to launch, it takes off like a rocket.

The same applies for your money when you save and invest. The sooner you start, the better the results will be in the long run, because of compounding. This doesn't mean that if you're forty or fifty, that you have missed, out. It just means that you may need to contribute a bit more, than someone who is in their twenties or thirties, in order to achieve the same results.

With this compounding equation in mind, I sat down one day and calculated what would happen if I was to save $100 per week and invest it over twenty years. My reason for doing this, was because I had read all about saving and investing and about compounding interest, yet I was sceptical and not convinced that making these sacrifices now (by way of missing out on fun stuff), would really make a difference in the long term. It took me about half an hour to calculate, but I must say, it was the best thirty minutes that I have spent, because it changed my mindset completely.

The key to this concept is to see how amazing your life would be financially in the future, rather than only focussing on the now. Let's take that $100, that I found by cutting back on lunches and coffees and see how the power of compounding works. Annually, $100 per week, equates to $5,200. Let's say that we invest that amount over twenty years, earning interest at a rate of 10% annually. In this case, we *don't* keep adding more money to our investment. We just save $5,200 and don't touch it for twenty years.

Wealth

To some, 10% may seem ambitious, but when invested correctly, which I will demonstrate shortly as part of a diversified portfolio, is very achievable. Let me clarify something important first. If we earnt 10% on $5,200, that would give us $520 in interest per year. The incredible thing about compounding, is, that it compounds on the interest as well as the original $5,200. For example, in the first year, we earn $520 interest. Add that to the $5,200 that we started with and now we have $5,720. Now we are earning interest on the entire $5,720 and not just the $5200. As I mentioned a moment ago, you can't spend the interest earnt. You must leave it, because this is where the power of compounding occurs.

If you were to invest that $5,200 over twenty years and not touch it, with the power of compounding, it would be worth $34, 983 in twenty years' time. Not bad for a few small sacrifices for just one year. This next part, is where I got excited and finally got it, when it came to delaying gratification. Let's say that you were going to continue saving $100 per week and invest that additional amount, each year, over ten years. With the power of compounding, the results are incredible.

Below is a table illustrating how your $100 per week, will grow over ten years using the power of compounding.

	OPENING BALANCE	AMOUNT INVESTED	INTEREST EARNED	CLOSING BALANCE
YEAR 1	$0	$5,200	$520	$5,720
YEAR 2	$12,012	$5,200	$1,092	$12,012
YEAR 3	$5,200	$5,200	$1,721	$18,933
YEAR 4	$18,933	$5,200	$2,413	$26,546
YEAR 5	$26,546	$5,200	$3,174	$34,921
YEAR 6	$34,921	$5,200	$4,012	$44,133
YEAR 7	$44,133	$5,200	$4,933	$54,266
YEAR 8	$54,266	$5,200	$5,946	$65,413
YEAR 9	$65,413	$5,200	$7,061	$77,674
YEAR 10	$77,674	$5,200	$8,287	$91,162

CREATE THE LIFE YOU WANT

As you can see, your $100 per week, which would otherwise be $52,000, has now grown to $91,162 in ten short years through the power of compounding. That's $39,162 in interest that you have earnt over that time.

Here's where it gets even better. In the next three lots of five years, your money almost doubles every five years.

By year 15, your $100 per week, would be worth - $181,738
By year 20, your $100 per week, would be worth - $327,612
By year 25, your $100 per week, would be worth - $562,545

Please note that these figures are only an estimate and are based on average returns of 10% per year. These calculations are for example purposes only.

Not only, do you now have more than half a million dollars, but on top of that, by year 25, you are earning $51,140 per year in *interest alone*. In other words, you could take out that much each year and not be eating into your capital. If you are around my age (44) and planning on retiring in around twenty-five years, then $51,140 per year, will be a nice start.

When I did this for my own situation and saw these figures, it blew my mind. It also made me realise, that just by making a few simple changes to my life, I too could create an income stream for when I retire. I personally could live with a few small sacrifices, to achieve those sorts of results in the future.

Key principle number five: Invest the difference

Hopefully by now, you will be inspired to find those extra savings and be willing to build wealth for your future. So far, I have explained how to have a better relationship with money, how to spend less than you earn and how to have a good budget. We then looked at the power of compounding. Now it's time for the best part, which is to take the money that you've saved (by spending less than we earn), and invest the difference.

At this point, I must be clear that earning 10% per year is not going to happen, by putting your money in the bank and leaving it. With the cost of

Wealth

inflation and low interest rates, your money would actually go backwards over twenty years, if left in a bank.

"Oh great," you say. "Get my hopes up, then cut me down." Not quite. There is a way to earn 10% returns per year, without having to gamble or take excessive risks. By building a diversified portfolio of investments, it is realistic to achieve 10% returns on average over the long term. Many investors obtain returns, well in excess of 20% per year, so 10% is actually conservative.

This key principle can seem very scary to most people and for good reason. I too was someone, who had absolutely no clue how to invest, how the stock market worked, or even how to buy stocks. Thankfully, with the age of the internet, there are so many great resources, when it comes to investing, that can help you on your journey. As long as you have the right attitude towards money, you will find a way. I will however, guide you through some easy to use ways in this book too.

As I have previously stated, this is **not** an area that you want to leave up to someone else to take care of. Yes, if you know a reputable financial advisor, who you trust, then by all means, have them guide you, but I urge you to display a great amount of caution, when engaging a financial advisor or an investment broker.

There are many great financial planners and many who are sincere, but as Tony Robbins said, someone can be sincere and be sincerely wrong. The most important thing, is that whether you do it yourself, or have a financial advisor do it for you, make sure that you understand the entire process and what is happening to your money; along with the risks associated with this. There has been so much research conducted, that has proven beyond a shadow of a doubt, that for the most part, financial planners and stock brokers are *not* able to provide their clients with superior results, to that which the client could gain on their own.

This is precisely why I strongly recommend that you take a proactive interest in your own financial affairs. This is what I did and I am glad I did. I have read almost one-hundred books on investing and as a result, I am able to confidently navigate and understand how to safely invest. I don't claim to know everything, but I want you to know, that I started out knowing nothing and now confidently invest as well as someone that I would pay to do the work for me.

I am not saying that you will only know enough to invest, once you have read as many books as me. That's why I wrote this book, so that you don't have to sift through as many books as I did. My hope, is that by the end of this chapter, along with the other finance books that I recommend, you too will be able to confidently navigate this part of your life.

At the end of the book are my favourite finance related books, that will give you confidence to begin your own investing journey. Each one of these books gives you easy to understand and easy to apply methods, for transforming your financial situation. These books provide different information, but the one thing that they, along with almost every single investing book ever written agrees on, is that in order to achieve your desired results, you must diversify your investments.

My father was a well-known accountant in our city when I was growing up. Our city was quite small, with only 150,000 people when I was younger, so dad was everyone's accountant. One regret of mine, was that I had no interest in money growing up, so I was not able to benefit from his incredible wealth of knowledge, when it came to money and investing.

One thing that I do remember Dad saying though, was that if you want to be assured of winning in the game of investing, *you must diversify*. He explained to me that you can't just put all of your money into the bank, or put all of your money into a house and not have anything else. His reasoning for this, was quite simply. If you have all of your eggs in one basket, and something happens to that basket, you could lose everything.

This line of thought is echoed in every one of the finance book that I have read, by some of the greatest minds in the world of investing. People like Warren Buffet, Ray Dalio, Phil Town, Robert Kiyosaki, Tony Robbins and many others, all agree that you must diversify.

Most people are scared of investing, because they have either heard horrors stories of people losing all their wealth, or they themselves have lost everything. In many cases where this has occurred, it has happened

Wealth

from a lack of diversification, or a lack of education. In 2009 when the stock market crashed, the only savings I had, were as a part of my employer provided superannuation (Or 401K / Roth IRA, as they call them in the USA).

When the stock market crashed in 2009, like most people, my superannuation took a huge hit too. I didn't have a large amount to lose in the first place, but none the less, on paper, I lost a lot of what I did have. This made me realise what I confirmed years later, that most professionals investing our money, are as bad as the rest of us, when it comes to protecting our wealth.

What it also taught me, was that if I wanted to avoid that gut-wrenching feeling, that I had when I saw my superannuation statement with 20% less money in my account, was that I needed to take control and learn how to not let that happen again. Through reading the books that I read, I now know that the answer is diversification. This is not to say that even with a diversified portfolio, that you won't take a hit now and then, but if done correctly, that hit will be much smaller than most people, who don't diversify.

To create a well-diversified portfolio, you must spread your money across different asset classes. What this does, is act like a metaphoric bed of nails for your investments. We all know that if we were to lay on one single nail pointing upwards, or even four or five nails, they would all pierce through our skin, at the point of contact. On the other hand, if we were to place thousands of nails pointing upwards and lay down on them, the impact would be spread sufficiently, so that no single nail, nor the collection of nails, would make any impact; other than a small mark.

Creating a diversified portfolio, works in the same way. By spreading the risk, we decrease the chance of damage. For example, many people buy a home and put all of their savings into paying it off. They then buy another investment property, or even a few. This is a great plan, however, if the property market crashes, they stand to lose a lot of money. You might be thinking that house prices only go up though. Well that isn't entirely true. For the most part, yes, house prices do go up, but there have been occasions, where there have been crashes in the market, so it is still a better idea to not put all of your money into that asset class.

Just to clarify, the main asset classes that you should invest in to create a balanced or diversified portfolio are:

Property (Or property investments such as Real Estate Investment Trusts)
Cash (Or cash equivalents)
Bonds
Shares (Both domestic and International)
Commodities (such as Gold, Oil, etc.)

Each of these asset classes, for the most part, fluctuate independently of each other. For example, what this may mean, is that if there is a crash in the housing market, then generally, shares won't be affected, in the same way. If interest rates go up, earning you more interest on your cash investments, bonds will generally go down. Very rarely will all of these asset classes move in the same direction, at the same time. There may be some correlation, but generally, they will move independently.

By having your investments spread across some, or all of these assets classes, you will maximize the upside, while protecting against the downside. If the stock market crashes and you lose a big chunk of your investments in shares, your bonds or property will more than likely move upwards, or remain steady. Making sure that you diversify, is key to succeeding in providing for your future. The idea of a diversified portfolio is not one where all of the assets go up together. If this was to happen, then there is every likelihood, that they will all go down together too. A well-diversified portfolio will usually have some assets up, and others moving down, at any given time. That is how it is supposed to work and how it protects against big losses.

My father had a well-diversified portfolio. When he died, aged 91, my brother was the executor of his estate and began dismantling all of dad's investments. What my brother found, surprised me, because given that dad was 91, I would have thought (and hoped) that he had spent all of his money and had very little left at the time of his death. Not only did dad

Wealth

not run out of money at age 91, but he still had quite a portfolio of investments, that well and truly outlived him. This proved beyond a shadow of a doubt to me, that a well-diversified portfolio of investments, is a must, if you want to be wealthy and not run out of money.

Key principle number six: Creating a diversified portfolio

There are many schools of thought on what is the best way to create a well-diversified portfolio. Some say that it all depends on your age, some say it depends on your risk profile and others profess that there is a "one size fits all" approach of 30% bonds and 70% stocks. These strategies all have their merits and all have flaws.

Many investors say, "Never put all of your eggs in one basket", whereas Warren Buffett says, "Put all your eggs in one basket, then watch that basket very carefully". Unless you're Warren Buffett though, or have his incredible analytical mind, then you should pretty much rule out his strategy.

As I mentioned in the previous key principle, diversifying across various assets classes is a must, when trying to protect against loss. While diversifying is a must, the trap some investors make, is to *over diversify* their portfolio. It has been proven in many studies, that there is a limit of where diversification stops being of benefits. By this I mean, that having one stock in your portfolio, could have a standard deviation of 50%. Increasing your portfolio to eight stocks, will reduce that standard deviation to 25%, but increasing your portfolio to twenty stocks, may only reduce it to 22%. Once you reach a certain point of diversifying, there is no longer the same benefit.

Let's look at the strategy that I use, which is similar to the template that I learnt from Tony Robbins and Ray Dalio. Ray Dalio is the fund manager of Bridgewater Associates, which is one of the largest hedge funds in the world. Ray's track record in all types of markets is almost unrivalled. Ray believes that the best approach, is to have parts in your portfolio that move separately and essentially in different directions. Some of the parts move fast, in one direction, while others move slowly, either in the same direction, or opposite. Thus, eliminating major losses.

At the time of writing this book, I am forty-four so I am in the middle of where most people begin their investing journey. I am not in my twenties, so I can't be too reckless, however, I am not approaching retirement just yet, so I don't need to be too overly cautious either. I want a portfolio that will grow at a reasonable rate, while not being overly volatile to risky markets.

Picking individual stocks, is something that many profess to be good at; but very few are. When I say, very few are, I am also talking about most fund managers and to some extent; myself. Picking individual stocks is a fairly small percentage of my portfolio and it is not something that I recommend for the average investor. The fact that professional fund managers and stock brokers fail miserably at this, illustrates that picking stocks is not as easy as they would lead us to believe. Of my overall portfolio, only 31% is made up of individual companies.

To give you an idea of what I believe to be a well-diversified investment portfolio, I have broken down my own portfolio, which I modelled on an "All Seasons portfolio" that Ray Dalio provided to Tony Robbins, in "Money, Master the game". I have changed it to suit my own needs and just like Ray, I am confident that it will fare much better than many other types of portfolios; in all markets. The below portfolio does not include my superannuation (or 401K for Americans). My superannuation operates separately and I have different investments allocations for my super.

This is what my portfolio looks like:

1. 19% - Cash
2. 15% - Australian shares ETF (ASX200)
3. 7% - International shares ETF (Worldwide - excluding USA)
4. 7% - USA Small cap (individual company)
5. 7% - USA Large cap (individual company)
6. 12% - R.E.I.T (ETF)
7. 9% - Bonds (ETF)

Wealth

8. 7% - Gold (individual company)
9. 7% - Resources stocks (individual company)
10. 10% - Healthcare stocks (individual company)

This portfolio gives me a great mix of assets across different asset classes, with varied correlation, which will see my portfolio weather almost any situation. These percentages have been calculated based on my age, risk tolerance and what I believe to be the best approach towards good diversification. The benefit of this portfolio, is that while I may miss out on the highest of gains occasionally, I will be less likely to suffer the worst of losses, as a result.

So, let's break it down.

1. Cash / Cash equivalents – 19%

I strongly recommend that you hold at least 10 – 20% of all your total portfolio in cash. There are several reasons for this. Firstly, this is for safety, should you suffer a loss through a stock market crash, or a downturn in the housing market. It will also provide stability, in the event of a job loss. It is suggested by many experts that you have at least six months cash reserves at any time for safety. This is debatable, but I do suggest at least two months wages in cash supply, as a minimum.

The 10 – 20% in cash, is an absolute minimum, because if you're working towards an investment plan (which everyone should have), then you will more than likely have extra cash in hand, depending on the market at the time. I currently have closer to 40% in cash at the time of writing this book, because we are going through a sustained "bull market", so the majority of shares are way over priced and not worth buying; in my opinion.

I have this cash on hand, so that when the market takes a correction, or a crash (which will happen), I am ready to pounce and buy some undervalued stocks. As much as most investors think that they have the mindset and courage to hold shares when they crash; most don't. For most people, having 10% cash is sufficient, but because I am always on the lookout for an undervalued stock, I like to keep more on hand, so that I can act quickly, when I see something I want to invest in, for a bargain price; without leaving myself with no cash.

For the past five or six years, Warren Buffett has had billions of dollars in cash reserves, because he too believes that most stocks are overpriced. Many people see a stock market crash as a bad thing, when in fact, it is a wonderful opportunity. Warren Buffet is one of the greatest proponents of this, as he patiently waits for a stock market crash, so he can charge in like a bull in a china shop. Most people think that you make money on the stock market or in property when you sell, but the truth is, that you make the money when you buy. The price you pay when buying stocks or property, will determine your level of profit when you sell.

Therefore, its strongly advised to hold an amount of cash, so that you can capitalise on a stock market crash, or downturn. If you already own some shares in a company and they have a correction (a downturn or 10% or more), then this is a great time to buy more of the same stock. By purchasing more shares at the lower price, it will bring down your average price per share and therefore lead to greater profits when you sell them in the future. This is providing that you have done your research and you are sure that the company is a good one. Don't just ride out the losses and wait for them to go back up. When the price of shares you hold goes down significantly, buy more. This is why having cash ready, is so important to creating wealth.

There are schools of thought that borrowing to purchase shares can be a good way to get ahead. I see merit in this approach, but only if you know exactly what you are buying and you are 200% sure that it is going to increase in value. When "leveraging" (Borrowing) to buy stocks, if you make a good choice, your profit increases, but if you lose, you lose bigger, so I urge caution to this approach.

2. Domestic shares – 15%

Because I am not Warren Buffett (and neither are you), I recommend predominately using low-cost "index funds" for most of your investment portfolio. Index funds, or ETF's (Exchange Traded Funds), are funds that "mimic" certain categories of stocks, to obtain comparable results.

For example, if you want to invest in every company listed on the American Stock Exchange (N.Y.S.E), it would cost you millions of dollars. An easier and cheaper way, is to invest in an index fund, that mimics the "Russell 3000", which is every stock listed on the NYSE. Companies such as Blackrock investments or Vanguard Investments, have such index funds and for a very small fee, you can have access to all of these stocks.

The reason for me recommending index funds over "managed funds" is for the following reason. Index funds have much lower fees than managed funds and while you may not think that a 1% or 2% will make much difference, I can assure you, that over twenty years, it could be a difference of hundreds of thousands of dollars.

Managed funds have higher fees because they are "managed". In other words, fund managers spend a lot of time, buying and selling stocks inside the fund, as they try to "beat" the market, to gain superior returns for their investors. Because managed funds have higher fees, your actual gain, ends up being lower. Index funds have much less buying and selling, so therefore have much lower fees. It has been proven through numerous studies, that the success rate of fund managers beating the market, is extremely low, so why pay them extra fees, if you're not receiving a bigger profit?

The 15% that I have in Australian shares, is in an index fund that mimics the ASX200, which is the index monitoring the top 200 companies listed on the Australian Stock Exchange. For me to buy shares in the top 200 publicly listed companies in Australia individually, would cost me millions of dollars. An index fund that is very similar to this, acts and moves, almost identically to the ASX200. It is much cheaper to purchase and has very low management fees, so it's a great option for everyday investors.

This index fund, generally moves the same as the ASX200, so it reflects very similar gains and losses of the ASX. While you may not "beat the market", using this approach, you certainly won't get slaughtered by it either. Your returns will be very similar to the index that the fund is mimicking. If the market has a good year, so will you and vice versa.

CREATE THE LIFE YOU WANT

Vanguard Investments, Blackrock Investments and BetaShares, all have a good varieties of index funds that cover most asset classes. They all have low fees and are a great way for regular investors.

Vanguard: www.vanguardinvestments.com.au
Blackrock: www.blackrock.com/au
BetaShares: www.betashares.com.au

The websites listed above, are Australian sites, however, these companies all have head offices in the USA and overseas, so they are large companies and have websites for each region. I recommend that take time to go through all of their ETF's and other funds that they have. Make sure that you read all of the product disclosure statements and supporting documentation, when considering your investments options. Like anything that you buy, you must do research on any investment product, so that you fully understand it, before making a decision.

While I personally like these funds and the "index approach" to investing, this investment advice is general in nature, so I strongly recommend that you talk to an investment advisor, or do your own thorough research before purchasing any of these products.

3. International shares – 7%

Inside your portfolio, I recommend having a mixture of domestic and international shares. Having a mix of both, gives you more opportunity for growth as well as protecting you against complete losses if one particular market crashes.

The Australian and US markets do share some common influencing factors and can move in the same direction. These factors, which tend to be world events, can affect both domestic and international indexes simultaneously, however, they are separate identities and generally move at varied rates. This is why I have a mix of both domestic and international shares through index funds, to spread my risk, while giving me exposure to different markets around the world.

Wealth

As well as domestic shares, I have 7% of my portfolio invested in international shares. This is by way of another index fund, that follows the worldwide index; *excluding USA*. This index fund includes every market around the world, but *not* the USA. The reason why I have kept the NYSE (New York Stock Exchange) separate, is the NYSE moves differently to the rest of the world. In other words, If the NYSE encounters a crash, my worldwide index, won't be as greatly affected as it would be, if I included the NYSE in my worldwide index.

4. USA: Small Cap – 7%
5. USA: Large Cap – 7%

When it comes to US stocks, I have broken them up into small cap and large cap stocks, of which I have 7% of each. My recommendation on this, is because the N.Y.S.E, is one of the biggest markets in the world. It is therefore, one with a lot of potential for growth. On the other side of the equation, it is also the one, that could be most affected by volatility. It is for these reasons, that I recommend, further diversifying into small and large cap stocks, so you can benefit the most.

Small cap stocks are companies that have a market capitalisation of between $300 Million to $2 Billion. Small cap stocks, historically tend to grow faster than large cap stocks, but tend to be more volatile. Large cap stocks are companies with a market capitalisation of $10 Billion or more. Large cap stocks grow more slowly, but are far less volatile.

The balance between the two, gives a good mix of growth and stability, while both capitalising on this exciting market. If you are younger and don't mind more risk, then you may want to balance this part of your portfolio with more small cap stocks, or even go with 10-15% of each and reduce your percentage of another part of your portfolio. If you're edging closer to retirement and safety is more your concern, then larger cap stocks might be more to your liking.

Large cap stocks are like the main meal, while small cap stocks are like dessert. The main meal is nutritious and good for us, but we all want to fill up on dessert. Truth be known that if we do, we might explode; just like your portfolio. That is why I recommend a mix of both, so you can have the best of both worlds.

This part of your portfolio, will tend to be where the biggest gains are. There is more risk of losses here too, but for the most part, this portion will really push your portfolio along at a rapid rate. With this part of my portfolio, I choose individual companies to invest in. Even though choosing individual companies can be risky, this is a small part of my portfolio, so it isn't as big a risk, as it would be, if my entire portfolio was made up of individual stocks.

When choosing companies to invest in for this part of my portfolio, I use a fairly simple approach. I use a financial search site, such as Yahoo Finance, or Google Finance and look for companies that are performing well, but are under-priced. Everyone wants the next Amazon, or Facebook stock, so they tend to jump in, when the prices are rising. The problem with that though, is that by the time, you hear that it is an awesome stock, the price has gone up so much, that it is no longer a good buy.

As I mentioned earlier, you never pay full price for anything, so buying shares is the same. Yes, buying a great company like Amazon, will provide you with good profits, for a long time, but there is always a possibility that it may crash. If you paid too much for it, then when that crash comes, it will take a lot longer for the price to recover, than if you bought it for a cheaper price.

When I am looking for a company to invest in, I look for the following. I want a company that has a solid record of growth and I want it to have a small amount of debt. While debt can be a sign of growth with a company, for simplicity, I like the debt to equity ratio to be below *1*. This indicates that the company could easily pay off its debt, if it needed to.

I also want a company that has a high R.O.I (Return On Investment), a high R.O.E (Return On Equity) and a good R.O.C (Return On Capital). These three indicators, show that the company is good at investing their money, in all areas. For me, if they have these three indicators at 20% or above, as a minimum, then that is a good start. I tend to go for stocks that

Wealth

have these indicators at over 30%, though. In particular, I want to see that the R.O.C is also increasing each year; not decreasing.

In addition, I want to see that the company is either at the top of its sector; or very close. For example, if it is a healthcare company, then I want the above indicators, to be better than their competitors. All of these comparisons, can be done on sites such as Google Finance. Another important thing that I look for is, I want the company to have a low P/E (Price to Earnings ratio). For me, I prefer the P/E to be less than 10, but definitely no more than 15.

Sites such as Google Finance, show the P/E ratio, but if you want to calculate it yourself, you simply take the share price and divide it by the EPS (Earnings Per Share). For example; If the share price is $4.00 and the EPS is 0.2, then the P/E = 20. One of the companies that I invest in has a share price of $2.98 and an EPS of 0.3. This gives me a P/E of 9.93, which is well within my target range. The company's debt to assets is 0.9 (under my target of 1) The ROC is 25.5%, ROI is 29.1% and the ROE is 41.37%. This means that the company fits the criteria for me to buy it and will provide me with a good return into the future.

At the other end of the spectrum, let's take Facebook as an example. Facebook is a profitable company and is providing shareholders with good profits, however, to buy into Facebook now (at the time of writing this book), would be ludicrous. Facebook has a price per share of $180.06. It's Earnings per share are $4.60. So, in other words, for every share that the company has outstanding, it is earning $4.60. If we divide the share price by the EPS, it gives us a P/E of 39.11. In my opinion, this is way too high to be buying in. If I was to buy Facebook shares, it would have to have a large decline in price, to somewhere around $92.00 as a maximum (20 x $4.60 EPS). Even that would be quite high, by my calculations.

If I find a company that meets all of the criteria that I want, it doesn't mean that I buy it. It has to be at the right price. For me, if the stock is selling for less than 2/3 of its intrinsic value, or if it is selling for a P/E of between 10-15 then I buy it. If not, then I monitor it, until it is. This might take weeks, or months, but it is essential that you don't pay too much for it, regardless of how good the company is. If you are going to purchase shares in company that does have a higher P/E than 20, then you need to make sure that it is a very reputable company, with very good long-term growth.

When doing research on companies to invest in, always visit the company's investor website. Although it may seem boring to do so, you need to take some time to at least look through the company's annual reports and financial statements. The more you understand about the company that you are investing in, the better chance you have of making the right choice.

When building your portfolio, I am not suggesting that you try to "time the market". While you don't want to pay too much for a stock, you don't want to be sitting on the side lines either. I do suggest being patient, but at the end of the day, you are better getting in, than sitting on the side line. It is *"time in"* the market; not *"timing"* the market, that is the key to success in investing.

If you do happen to jump in and stock prices go down, that is ok. Providing that you have done your research and the company is good, then buy more. If you buy more shares at the lower price, this will bring your average price per share down and therefore increasing your returns, once the share price goes back up. One thing to note, is that if you are buying additional stock to top up what you already own (or even when purchasing initial shares), it is better to buy more "units", than less. Each transaction that you make, when buying or selling shares, will incur a brokerage fee. This fee is usually $20 for the average private investor when purchased through an online broker.

This fee can make a big difference to the overall price per share, when you purchase. For example: If you buy 1,000 shares of company "XYZ", at $3.00 per share, the total cost of the transaction (including brokerage fee) will be $3,020. This means that the price you pay per share, is $3.02 and not $3.00. That is not a big difference, but if you buy 100 shares at $3.00 per share, when you calculate your fee into the equation, your cost is $3.20 per share. This means that your company will need to increase by 20 cents per share, for you to even be square. Keep this in mind, when buying or selling shares, as it can make a big difference, in the end. If possible, it is better to buy 2000 shares in one transaction, rather than 4 x 500 shares.

The strategy I mentioned earlier, about buying a stock at 2/3 of its intrinsic value, is what Warren Buffett and his mentor, Benjamin Graham refer to as having a "margin of safety". By having a margin of safety, you are insuring yourself against price decreases, which will occur. Remember, the lower the price you pay for a share, the more profit you make, when you sell it.

If you want to learn more about how to buys stocks, with a margin of safety, I highly recommend Benjamin Graham's books; "The intelligent investor" and "Security Analysis". These books go into great depth, on this strategy that has made Buffett the world's greatest investor. I really just wanted to give you a taste of this concept, so that you have an understanding of it. As I have previously stated, if it is something that is too complex for you, or you just want a simpler approach, then there are suitable index funds that you can invest in, that are far less complex.

6. R.E.I.T's – 12%

My next 12% of my portfolio, is invested in R.E.I.T's. A R.E.I.T is a Real Estate Investment Trust and is a stock (or index fund) that invests solely in real estate. This can include, commercial, industrial or residential property; or a combination of all of them. At this stage, I do not own a property (for reasons I will explain shortly), so this is how I invest in real estate. You can own R.E.I.T's as well as a home, or one or the other.

Some investors have a home and an investment property and some have neither. It is recommended that every portfolio has some type of real estate investment, for diversity. R.E.I.T's are completely different from other shares, because they invest predominately in property, so therefore react to market fluctuations differently to other domestic or international shares. Having R.E.I.T's or property, is a great way to balance your portfolio.

R.E.I.T's can be invested in as individual stocks, or through an index fund, same as other shares that you can buy. The returns on REIT's tend to be much higher than bonds and cash, but they are more stable than shares.

7. Bonds – 9%

I recommend 9% as a minimum for bonds in any portfolio. Bonds move very differently to stocks and R.E.I.T's, so there are an important part of having a "safe" portfolio. Most investors who are entering into their retirement years will hold anywhere from 50% - 80% in bonds. This is because of the bond's stability and the regular coupon payments, that they receive by holding bonds. This creates a regular income stream which many older investors desire. Bonds will not provide the same level of returns as shares, or REIT's, but they will provide much more stability to your portfolio.

A bond is a debt security, like an IOU. Borrows issue bonds to raise money for new projects. The most common types of bonds are, treasury bonds, government bonds and corporate bonds. I'm reluctant to get too deep into talking too much about bonds, simply because I could honestly fill an entire new book on bonds alone. I must also confess, that bonds are one area that I myself am still learning about (I told you this was the "no bullshit" book). My main objective, is that you understand what bonds are and how they can play an integral part of your portfolio.

If you wish to look further into bonds, I highly recommend doing more research. A great place to start is http://www.asx.com.au/products/bonds.htm

What I will tell you, is that historically, bonds move very differently to stocks. This provides your portfolio with less overall volatility and therefore greater potential returns. Generally, when interest rates go down, (which helps you to pay off your mortgage quickest, if you wish to), bonds go up in value. The opposite generally occurs with bonds, when interest rates go up. This is not a hard and fast rule, but it is the case, more often, than not. Bonds react differently to world events, to stocks, so while you may take a hit if your stocks go down, your bonds will mostly go in the opposite direction; albeit not as dramatically.

A bond is purchased at an agreed rate, for an agreed duration. Over the course of that duration, the borrower, agrees to pay a "coupon" to you (twice a year, or quarterly), which is a percentage amount (5% as an example). This is essentially interest that they are paying you, for lending them the money. At the end of the term (maturity), you receive your initial outlay back as well. If, however, you decide to sell your bonds prior to maturity, the price that is paid could have decreased or increased. This price will be determined by the movement of interest rates.

While bonds, are more stable that stocks, they don't have the same potential growth (or loss) as stocks either. While stocks may grow by 12% - 30% in a year, bonds may only grow by 2% - 5%. On the flipside, stocks could decline by 20%, whereas bonds, will only decline by 5%. It is for these reasons, that I strongly recommend that you hold bonds as part of.

The amount of bonds, you hold depends on many factors, such as your age, your financial goals and your risk tolerance. I found out first hand that my risk tolerance is not as high as I thought, when I started investing. Most people are the same as me. They think they would be ok, if they suffer losses, but when it happens, they freak out and sell everything.

Because bonds are a completely different animal to stocks, I have chosen a simple approach to investing in bonds. I have my 9% invested in a bond index fund. This fund takes a stake in a large variety of bonds, that spread across Australian treasury and government bonds. If you wish to diversify further, there are bond index funds that also spread across different countries and even include more risky types of bonds.

I have taken this simplistic approach, because I didn't have the desire to sift through thousands of individual bonds. To work out which ones were the best. When I began researching bonds, I quickly discovered that there are many more types of bonds, than there are different items in a supermarket. For the average investor, this can be extremely daunting, trying to work out what is the best option. I also felt that having a fund that invests in a broad range of bonds, gave me the stability that I needed, without the huge costs (and risks) associated with me buying lots of separate bonds.

8. Gold – 7%
9. Commodities / Resources stocks – 7 %

    In Tony Robbin's "Money, master the game", Ray Dalio explains that he recommends having a mix of Gold & Commodities in a portfolio. To some investors, gold is something shinny that does nothing, but to others, it's an important piece of the puzzle. Because commodities prices usually rise when inflation is accelerating, they offer protection from the risks of inflation.

    In my portfolio, I have 7% invested in a Gold producing company and 7% invested in a Resources index ETF. I used the same formula that I used to pick small and large cap stocks, to find a suitable under-priced company than is in the gold sector, while I kept it simple, so far as resources, by choosing a low-s cost index fund.

10. Healthcare – 10%

For the last part of my portfolio, I have allocated 10% to healthcare stocks. With the aging population around the world, this sector, is one that looks to be on the rise, well into the future.

    I found a healthcare company that was way under-priced, yet it was out performing all of its competitors in the healthcare sector. When choosing a suitable healthcare stock, I used the same formula for choosing shares. If however, you want to take a most simplistic approach, there are once again index funds (ETF's) that can give you exposure to this sector, for very little cost.

    All the pieces of my investment portfolio are either great value companies, or low cost index funds, all of which I can buy or sell myself, on my online trading account. When I started investing, I had no idea how I could start. I had enough information that I knew what I wanted to buy, but I had no experience as to how to buy them.

    As I mentioned earlier, while it is not recommended to time the market, you do want to choose, what you buy and when. Try to use a little "timing" when buying the individual parts of your portfolio, so you don't pay too much, but so far as the index funds, you are better off, just getting in. At the end of the day, the most important thing, it that you are investing.

In Tony Robbins' book "Unshakeable", Tony illustrates the pitfalls of the market timing approach. What I suggest (and what I did), is once you're confident of your portfolio choices, then buy your index funds and start monitoring your individual companies, until the price is right. Over the following weeks or months, when each of the other sectors or companies have a correction (downturn) of 10% or more, or if they are at a very attractive price, in relation to their performance, then you buy that piece of the puzzle.

The way I did this, was I found the companies that I wanted to invest in (after conducting thorough research), then I took notes of their current price and the date. That way I could monitor them daily, weekly, or monthly, until they reached a price that I was happy to pay for them. In some cases, I bought the stocks, while in other cases, I changed my mind about them prior to purchasing; based on my research.

Once you get more confident in investing, another great book on calculating the best price and value of stocks is "Rule #1" by Phil Town. This book, goes in to detail, as to how to value a company and create a margin of safety, so that you maximize the upside, while protecting against the downside.

The approach that I suggest, to create your portfolio, allows you to get into the market and not miss out, while not jumping in at the wrong time, or paying too much. It's not a perfect formula, but when it comes to the stock market, there is no such thing as a perfect formula. Anyone who tries to sell you a "perfect formula", should be avoided at all costs. Remember, we all make mistakes when it comes to investing, so take your time, do your research and if you screw up; learn from it.

There are various online brokers, who can help you, that are inexpensive and that provide you with support in setting up your account and placing orders to buy, or sell. I was surprised at just how easy it was to set up an account and start investing. If you're a little uneasy about placing your first purchase, most online platforms have a function where you can "pretend trade". This is where you have an allocated amount of pretend money and you can buy and sell shares, just like you normally would and then monitor them to gauge your level of decision making.

If you buy the wrong share and it goes down, it doesn't cost you, but if it goes up, you don't get to keep the money either. It is purely for practise purposes, so you can test yourself, before jumping in for real. The biggest thing with investing in anything, is to do your research. Just like buying a house or a car, you need to fully understand what you are buying. Warren Buffett is constantly saying that if he doesn't understand what a company does, then he doesn't buy it. My rule of thumb is, that if I can't explain what the company does to someone else, then I clearly don't know enough about it, to buy shares in it. It is important to know what you are investing in.

The best way to learn about stocks, is to get familiar with some of the free websites, such as Yahoo Finance, MSN Money and Google Finance. All of them are free and they have all the information you need to get started. I also recommend, subscribing to The Wall Street Journal or The Financial Review in Australia. Watch as many videos on YouTube and download all the podcasts that you can find.

There are thousands of ways to invest and everyone is different. What I would suggest though, is to avoid any "gimmick", or "the next big thing", that people push on you, such as bitcoins, or fad investments. These fads, are just that; fads. Just like pyramid schemes back in the day, the only people making money from them, are the ones who got in early, but even they are on borrowed time with their money. In the case of bitcoins, they are not yet regulated by anyone, so that in itself, is a dangerous proposition. If in the future, they are regulated, then perhaps, my mind will change on bitcoin. If you stick to tried and true methods of investing, you won't go too wrong, in the long term.

When it comes to investing, if it seems too good to be true; it usually is. Stick to strong investments, learn from the leaders in the industry, such as Warren Buffett and Ray Dalio and start slowly. You want to be buying shares, when everyone is selling. To go in the opposite direction to everyone else, is one of the hardest things anyone can do. It takes great courage

Wealth

and tenacity to be bold enough to stand alone and stand strong. In order to do so, you must first see what others don't see.

This won't occur by following the media or market analysts, because by the time they are speaking about it, or making recommendations, the big players have already made their move, so you've missed the boat. Take your time and do your research. Yes, I watch these shows and hear what they are saying, but not so I can follow their advice. Take advice from others, but make the decision yourself and don't let others influence you, because for the most part, they have their own motives for you to buy a product.

Throughout history, the majority of market crashes have occurred in times of greed and over-confidence. I heard Ray Dalio say just today, that you never learn anything from successes, but you learn a lot from failures; when combined with reflection.

When the market is thriving, people want to jump on board and cash in. Instead, you should be sitting back and thinking "it can't keep going this way forever". One of the oldest laws in the world is "what goes up; must come down".

It doesn't always happen when you expect it, or at the same time of a cycle, but the market will always correct itself, when it gets out of whack. When stocks are way overpriced and sentiment is high, this is the best time to be pessimistic. When everyone thinks that the sky is falling and the stock market is crashing; this is the time to be optimistic and bag a bargain.

Warren Buffett famously refused to buy tech stocks when the rest of the investing world seemed to be buying them. Analysts and commentators said that Warren had finally lost his edge, after so many years. Everyone thought that tech stocks would continue to ride the insane wave of gains, forever. Buffett stood strong, when everyone else were being sheep and following the herd.

Just as the masses were engraving Buffett's investing tombstone, the tech bubble burst in 2001 and most investors lost everything; but not Buffett. Warren Buffett, Ray Dalio and a handful of investors know that when everyone else is overconfident, they need to be cautious and when everyone else is pessimistic; they are overconfident.

Watch what the herd is doing; but don't follow them. If you're following the herd, there is a very good chance that you will be paying too much for the stocks, or selling at a loss. By the time you jump on board, the prices will be overinflated as a result of the big institutional investors and everyone else already buying in. Jumping on the band wagon late (once prices have risen), will lead to less than great gains (best case scenario) or huge losses, if they price has a correction.

The most important thing when it comes to investing, is for you to take charge of your own destiny. You may employ someone to do the work, but it is imperative that you know exactly what they are doing and understand the reasoning behind it.

I personally, would rather be in charge of my financial destiny. If I win, I celebrate, if I lose, I learn a valuable lesson. Either way; I win. When I started out on my financial journey, I knew nothing. I knew how to make money and spend money and make a basic budget, but that was it. I made the decision that I was no longer willing to live from week to week.

I became a student and as I began to learn, I realised how much I enjoyed learning all there was to know in this area. There is a misconception that finance and investing are hard to understand. It's not as bad as most people think. Yes, it takes a little time and effort to comprehend the complexities of the industry, but is there anything in life that is worth doing, that doesn't?

Like anything in life, if you want to be good at something, you must dedicate time to it. I succeeded in becoming a well-paid singer, travelling the world and I had no formal training, unlike most professional performers. I had a desire, found a way to learn my craft and then dedicated as much time and effort to that goal, as was required.

If you're not financially wealthy, it has nothing to do with bad luck, a poor family or anything, other than the fact that you are not committed to the goal of being financially successful. The good news is, that it is never too late to start and with some of the tools that I have shared with you in this chapter, I'm certain that you will succeed.

Key principle number seven: Rent verses buy.

Something that always sparks great debate in financial circles, is whether you should buy a home, or rent one. In Australia and around the world, there is a consensus that housing affordability is beyond the realm of most younger people. Whether or not this is the case, is not my focus here. I simply want to show you how to work out, if you wish to buy or rent, based on which option is best for you, financially.

For many years, so called experts have tried to tell us that "rent money is dead money". These are usually the banks who make a lot of money off us, if we lock in a mortgage for 25-30 years, so that's to be expected. I am not saying that in many instances, that this is not true (about rent money, being dead money), but let's look at it objectively and you can make your own decision.

Much research has been done over the years by financial analysts, which has proven that if you rent instead of buying a home, you will be better off in the long run. There is a catch to this though. The most important factor, is that if you decide to rent, instead of buying, then you *must* invest the difference, between what you mortgage payments would be and what you rent is.

The reason many people prefer to buy, is because it is what they call "forced savings". As previously mentioned, many people are bad at saving, so being locked into payments, means that in the long run, they will have a great asset, as well as a home to call their own. If you're a strong saver and an investor, then the money you can save by renting, can create a huge windfall in the long term and hence why this option is favoured by many financial analysts.

The outcome of this debate will have different results for everyone, so I don't want you to think that I am only suggesting one method over the other. What I want to do, is show you how I did my own calculations and came up with what worked best for me, in my current situation. Then I hope you will weigh up whether renting or buying is best for your own personal situation.

When I did this comparison, I was single, earning a single wage and living on my own. If you're married or a de-facto couple, then the results may turn out completely different, so make sure you do your own comparison based on how I did it. At the time of conducting the research, the security of owning my own home, was not as big a priority as those with a growing family.

I live in a three-bedroom house, with one bathroom and one car garage. I pay $370 per week in rent. To make an accurate calculation, I found a similar home nearby and found that the value of the home I was living in (along with the comparative home), were both around $440,000. When doing this comparison, you will need to find the price of a house in a similar neighbourhood, or a neighbourhood that you would like to buy in, to make these comparisons.

Let's presume that I had saved a 10% deposit ($44,000) for this home, so I am borrowing $396,000. Based on today's home loan interest rates, which are around 5.22% for a variable rate loan (Interest & principle), my weekly repayments on a $396,000 loan over 25 years; will be $592 per week. Keep in mind that at the time of writing this, interest rates in Australia, were at an all-time low. This is something that needs to be taken into account, because if interest rates were to rise (which they will sooner or later), then this will increase the amount between what mortgage payments would cost, and what your rent would be.

I believe that many families are already stretched beyond their means with their home loans, so the eminent rate rises in the future, may push this families beyond their means and thus costing them with the loss of their homes. It is essential that you factor in a "buffer" when calculating what you can afford, if buying a home, to ensure that you can handle any rate increases that lead to a hike in your repayments.

The difference between the $592 that I would be paying on a loan and the $370 in rent that I pay, is $222 per week. Over the course of the twen-

Wealth

ty-five-year loan, I would end up paying a total of $261,276 in interest alone. (This is providing that I make my payments weekly. If I make my repayments monthly, I would end up paying $313, 806 in interest over the period of the loan. This would mean that my $440,000 home, costs me $753,806 at the end of twenty-five years.

The average rate of return on properties will vary depending on where you live, but for this example, house prices have increased on average by 2.5% over the past twenty-five years. This means that your property will be worth $797,895. This gives you an overall return of $44,089 over twenty-five years. That is less than you 0.23% per year, which is worse than the lowest bank account available. I know that you will have a home to live in and potentially sell, but don't forget that you will need to buy another home, which will also cost more in twenty-five years. Based on this calculation, when it comes to investing, you would want much better returns on your money than that.

This of course is only an estimate, but it gives you an idea for the purposes of making an educated choice, as to which way is best for you. On top of your mortgage payments, you will need to factor in, council rates. Based on this property, council rates are $3,276 per year. This equates to $63 per week in addition to my loan repayments of $592, giving me a total of $655 per week in expenses to own your home.

If you look at the other side of the equation that I was looking at, my rent is only $370 per week. I don't have to pay council fees, so I have a difference of $285 between the cost of owning the property I live in, or renting. This $285 per week equates to $14,820 per year. If I was to invest that over twenty-five years, with an average rate of return of 10% compounding (As we learnt earlier), in twenty-five years, I would have a grand total of $1,478,423. I could now buy two homes with cash, with that sort of profit.

At that stage, I would also be earning a staggering $133,058 per year in interest alone. This amount in interest each year, would enough to live on; even if I had to pay rent still. Even with an inflation rate of 3% over the twenty-five years, $133K would be plenty to live on.

"But what about the fact that a home is an asset"?

CREATE THE LIFE YOU WANT

Well, that is not quite correct. As Robert Kiyosaki explained in his book, "Rich Dad, Poor Dad". A home is in fact, a liability; not an asset. A home is not an asset until it is paid off. The only part of the home that is an asset, is the equity that you own in the home. That too is not completely correct, because it is subject to you selling the home and finding a buyer willing to pay a price large enough to create that equity.

You may have a home that you think you have $50,000 equity in. You decide to sell it, but you receive $30,000 less that what you counted on. This means that you only have $20,000 equity as an asset. For the most part, a home does become an asset, but calculating it as such, when it's really a liability, only distorts your perception of your financial position. While real estate is a great long-term investment, unlike most investments, it is very hard for you to get your hands on your money, if you need to.

For me and my personal situation, this was a no brainer. For you, things may be different, based on your own personal situation. I simply wanted to show you, that you have more than one option and that you don't always need to believe the hype created by the money-making banks. If you have young family, then security may be of greater importance, so the stability of owning your own home may be a priority, but don't confuse this with investing.

Now, obviously, rent prices may increase over that time, but even if you factor in a 3% increase every five years, in my situation, I would still much better off renting. As I said earlier, this situation is one that works for me and my current situation, but this is also something that I will reassess, as things change and I urge you to do the same. If you are going to choose to rent, rather than buy a home, the key is to save / invest the difference, as explained. If you don't do this, then yes, rent money is dead money.

Key principle number eight: How much money do you really need?

Just like renting verses buying, there is so much debate over just how much money we need, in order to live comfortably in retirement. Everyone has a

Wealth

different opinion, a different percentage, a different dollar figure, but there really is no hard and fast answer to this question.

Like most people, I used to have a figure somewhere in the vicinity of one-hundred million dollars, that I felt that I needed in order to live happily into retirement. I had this idea that I needed a certain amount of money, to live the life I really wanted. When I actually sat down and calculated what it would take for me to be financially independent, the amount required, was so much less than I realised. What was even more astounding, was that when I sat down and calculated how much money I needed to live my wildest dreams, I was still not close to my original amount of roughly $100 million.

Unless you specifically want (or need) the most lavish house, a mammoth boat and a fancy private jet, you will be surprised just how little you need to live an amazing live in retirement. Let's face it, we all say that we want the above-mentioned house etc, but do you really? With all the maintenance costs and ongoing upkeep in comparison to the benefit of having such assets / liabilities, there is a much better and cost-effective alternative.

Tony Robbins has an exercise in one of his programs, where he talks you through a realistic guide to how much money you need, and surprisingly, it is not as much as you may think. The problem most people encounter, is that they work out how much their figure is with the huge house, boat and plane etc, then they realise that it is such a huge amount, that they say, "screw it", and don't even bother trying to achieve it.

Let's say that you want a huge super yacht to travel the world. The cost of such a vessel would start at $15,000,000 and could go up to $100,000,000. This is just the cost of purchasing the boat. You then need a full-time captain, which could set you back $80,000 per year at the very least. You will need to moor it somewhere and unless you have a waterfront home with a huge peer, then this can cost tens of thousands of dollars each year. On top of that, the cost of fuel and to maintain the vessel each year, would be more than two luxury family cars.

For most people (even in retirement), they would be lucky to travel for two months each year. If you were to charter the same vessel, in-

CREATE THE LIFE YOU WANT

stead of buying it, you could do so for eight weeks a year. The cost of this would start at around $15,000 per week, giving you a total cost per year of $120,000 and none of the expenses, or hassles of owning it. If you wanted to spend even more time traveling in a similar manor, you could book a cabin on board the Queen Victoria (One of the most luxurious ships in the world) for 134 nights, for $35,000 per person. This includes all your food and entertainment as well. This will take you all the way around the world in luxury, as you wished, but on a ship that which is much bigger and more stable, than a private boat.

The same is true with a private jet. Sure, it's a huge ego boost and convenience to have your own private jet. The reality is, that for a fraction of the cost of owning and maintain one, you can charter one as often as you like. Alternatively, you could fly first-class as often as you like and pay much less as well.

The point that I want to make here, is that you can live the life you want, without having to have as much money as you think you need. When I did Tony's exercise, I listed all the expenses that I would have, living my dream life in retirement and it worked out less than I thought. Below is an example of what I listed. Use this as an example and try it for yourself. I am sure that you too will be shocked at how little you really need.

Rent / Mortgage	$22,000
Council rates / taxes	$ 3,400
Groceries	$11,000
Bills ($250 / week)	$13,000
Spending ($230 / week)	$12,000
Clothing	$ 2,000
New car ($60k every 5 years)	$12,000
Holidays	$15,000
Donations	$10,000
Dinning out ($300 / week)	$15,600
TOTAL:	$116,000

Wealth

So, considering, all of my bills, expenses, spending, new cars every five years, holidays (flying business at that cost), dinning out and a new wardrobe each year, that is not a bad lifestyle, don't you think? For all of those things, it is still only $116,000 per year. I think you would agree, that this is not a bad lifestyle at all. You can up the amount for holidays, clothes etc if you wish. This is your dream life.

Let's say that you retire at 70 (which for most people, will be the age you are able to retire) and you live for another twenty years after retiring. To maintain that lifestyle, you would only need $2,320,000 total. If you owned your home by retirement (which is the case for most retirees), then you would only need $1,880,000 ($2,320,000 less 20 x $22,000).

This figure is much more realistic and more achievable than the$80,000,000 - $100,000,000 that I originally thought that I needed. Therefore, I am much more likely to go after this target. Even if I fall a bit short of my target, I am certain that I will be living well in retirement. I wanted to illustrate this to give you an idea of how it is possible to live a great lifestyle in retirement, so that you don't think that it is out of reach.

Take the time to list all the costs you would have living the life that you dream of. Make sure you list everything that it would take for you to live in a way that you never have to worry about money again. I think that you will be surprised at how little you will need to live an extraordinary life.

Once you have that figure worked out, then it's time to implement the strategies listed in this chapter for budgeting, cutting costs, saving & investing. These strategies will ensure that you reach that target in the future.

Ok, so now that we have you prepared to live a financially free lifestyle in retirement, let's look at how you are going to live long enough to enjoy the financial fruits of the above chapter.

Chapter Six

Health

> *"If all the medicine in the world, was thrown into the sea, it would be bad for the fish; but good for humanity."*
> —O. W Holmes

When it comes to living a happy life, no area can affect the outcome, more than your health. Money, career, family and relationships are all important, but if you're not healthy, then all the other areas of your life will suffer as a result.

The biggest issue with health these days, is that there is so much information available that is telling us what to eat, how to live and what we should and shouldn't be doing, to be healthy. I have personally found, that the best approach, is the simplest one. That is why I am going to keep things very simple in this chapter and help you to easily navigate your way to optimum health and wellbeing.

In the last ten years, I have been told by the Australian Medical Association (A.M.A) and other governing bodies, that eggs are bad for me, bananas are bad for me, coffee is bad for me, non-bottled water is bad for me, bacon is bad for me, meat is bad for me, sugar, salt, alcohol, chocolate, sunlight and a hundred other things that are a part of my life, are bad for me. It was about that same time (ten years ago), that I developed a "bullshit radar" when it came to what was bad for me.

I discovered that the one thing that *was* bad for me, was listening to these people and stressing about what was actually bad for me. Other than that, unless I indulged to a ridiculous excess of cigarettes, alcohol, fatty

Health

foods or drugs, that the biggest killer in my life, would be stress, from worrying about it.

This leads me to an important point. Stress will kill you more often than the foods you eat. The word "disease" is as it sounds, a "dis – ease" of the mind. The more you have dis-ease in the mind, the more susceptible you are, to allowing infections to enter your body. I am not suggesting that all you must do, is not stress and you will live until you're one-hundred, but by having a mind that is free of dis-ease, your body is more capable of fighting off infections and healing itself.

Diseases cannot live in an environment that is not conducive to them. If an infection enters a healthy body, it will more often than not, die off very quickly, because it does not have the environment that it needs to survive. It's like planting a plant. If the plant doesn't get water, sunlight and have good soil to grow in, it dies. Infections are the same. I can tell you from my own personal experience, that since I adopted a "less stressful" mindset, I have hardly been sick.

As I learnt many years ago, through Tony Robbins, our bodies are like a fish tank. I own tropical fish, so I know the importance of maintaining the correct levels in the tank. Just like the fish tank, our bodies are "acid & alkaline" based. If my fish tank gets too acidic, the fish are not able to live in that environment and they develop diseases and eventually die. We are the same. If our body get too acidic, it can no longer function properly. This includes fighting off toxins and infections, that we come into contact every day.

To maintain an environment that is able to fight off disease, you must be more alkaline, than acidic. Like most kids, I ate dirt, never washed my hands and I was unhygienic as a kid. Even though I'm sure my mother preferred that I wasn't quite so dirty, she knew that my body was building up an immune system and a healthy environment, by being this way.

When I was in pre-school, most kids were getting measles and chicken pox, but instead of keeping me away from these infectious kids, my mother made me hang out with them, so that my body could build up immunity as I grew. I guess that she realised pretty early on that I had a good immune system, because no matter how many infectious kids I hung out with, I didn't get any of their diseases.

One of the biggest causes of an acidic body, is stress. Because I want to keep this simple for you to understand, I won't get too in depth, but I do recommend that you listen to Tony Robbin's "Pure energy live" seminar on his "Get the edge" audio series. I also urge you to listen to and read any of Don Tolman's books or podcasts. Along with Wayne Dyer, Tony and Don, explain in depth, how powerful the body is at healing itself, if we give it the chance, by way of good nutrients and mindset.

When it comes to creating a healthy environment in our bodies, the biggest hurdle, is the rubbish information, that we are fed by big corporations, the media and the pharmaceutical industry. These three groups are your worst enemy, when it comes to your health. They do not have your best interests at heart. They are all about misleading you and creating propaganda, in order satisfy the interests of their shareholders and executives.

In most areas of my life, I am someone who is rarely negative or sceptical, but when it comes to health, I have developed a very healthy scepticism of the media and pharmaceutical industry; for very good reason. If you want to break free from disease, or be of optimum health, then I strongly urge you to adopt the same level of scepticism.

Unlike these industries, I have no agenda, no bias and no reason to relay this information to you; other than to provide you with the truth. In no way do I benefit from sharing this information, apart from knowing that I have helped you to break-free from the misleading information that is rammed down our throats every day.

It has always made sense to me, to embrace a different outlook towards my health, than that which has been forced upon society by these industries. My beliefs were backed up, when I met a true master of health; Don Tolman, a few years ago. These beliefs and lessons, were then reinforced when my own health improved because of this simple and common-sense approach.

The question we fail to ask, when it comes to money, fitness, or our health is; does it make sense? We are bombarded by information about foods, money etc and like obedient little sheep, we follow the herd, without any thought of whether or not it is right or wrong.

For thousands of years, humans lived long and healthy lives, by living as part of the earth. If you have any knowledge of quantum physics, you will understand, that the world is completely self-sufficient and so are all the parts that make up the earth. Humans and animals are designed in the same way that the earth is, so it therefore makes sense, that all we need is here already. All that we need to survive and thrive is contained in the earth. This does not include manufactured chemicals or enhanced substances; just products that are as close to their original natural source.

Both Don Tolman and Tony Robbins (along with many others), are very passionate about the fact that in order to thrive, we need to eat more foods that are alive. Most people eat foods that have nothing that is alive in them anymore. I am not here to push any agenda, such as vegan, paleo or fast food diet. I think that all the various lifestyles and diets, have their pros and cons. I just want to provide you with some good information, so that you can make the best choices for your own body. Doctors and nutritionists are highly skilled and for the most part, are sincere and mean well, but as I have stated before, someone can be sincere; and be sincerely wrong.

No one knows your body, better than you and if you listen to your own body, it will tell you what it needs. We live in such a fast-paced world these days, that we leave very little time for our health. Sure, most people workout at the gym for countless hours, but they then go and fill their bodies with endless amounts of chemically based pills / powders and wonder why they are getting sick.

Because of our lifestyles, health is the first area that suffers. We are not taking the time to organise good food for our bodies. When I look into people's shopping trolleys at the supermarket, I see tinned food, packaged food, junk food and very little real food. By real food, I mean, fruit, vegetables, meat and unprocessed foods. When it comes to our health, we have become so lazy. We buy packet dinners, packet lunches, protein bars, and instead of having a proper meal, we drink a chemically based protein shake.

CREATE THE LIFE YOU WANT

Right now, I've probably pissed off most dietitians and got many people off side, but what I am saying needs to be said. It's not made up by me. It has been proven over thousands of years. The only people disagreeing with this standpoint, are those who stand to lose out from people like me, Tony or Don exposing their lies and misleading information.

There is nothing in this chapter that isn't common sense and most of what I am writing, you already know. Unfortunately, over time, you may have been manipulated or mislead by big industries and have forgotten the simplest of facts, when it comes to nutrition. If you want to be healthy, be able to perform at your best and be disease free, then the first thing you need to do is ditch the processed foods, along with diet pills. In some cases, vitamin pills can assist in maintaining health, but not when they are used in the way that we are told to use them.

If you must use any form of vitamins, then please do so for short periods and only to *supplement* (not replace) your intake of that particular vitamin that you are lacking, until you are able to boost that vitamin through wholefoods. If you are lacking in any vitamin, you can easily find it, in its purest form, in living foods, rather than pills or powders. I am not totally against pills, powders or shakes, but only in very small amounts and as a temporary fix.

Vitamins and supplements are sold to us as a quick fix or solution to our dietary needs. Manufacturers of vitamins try to tell us that one little pill contains the same vitamin C as 500 oranges; WTF? What a load of bullshit! Not only is this not correct, but what they fail to tell you, is that in order to get the benefits of the vitamin C from the orange, you need the rest of the parts of the orange, which no longer exist in the pill, that you are taking. On top of that, the manufacturers have added a cocktail of poisons and chemicals to the pill, so that it has a shelf life long enough for it to be sold, without going bad.

Speaking of shelf life, in every processed packet food or tinned food that you buy, there are various chemicals added so the food doesn't go off. I'd love to get deep into this mess that corporations get involved in, but the book would be five-thousand pages long. I really just want to spell

Health

this out in the simplest of terms, so that you can break-free from their misleading marketing.

The bottom line when it comes to health, is that wholefoods and natural foods, that contain come living parts, are the best option for creating optimum health. As I said, I am not here to push any particular diet. Others dig deep into the benefits of eating meat, or not eating meat etc. I myself, have this simple approach. I eat a reasonable mix of wholefoods (fruits and vegetables) along with a small amount of meats (beef, chicken, lamb, pork) and grains and fats. I very rarely touch any form of processed food, tinned food or packaged food.

Because we are designed in the same image as everything around us, it makes sense that wholefoods provide our bodies with everything that they need. To listen to Don Tolman; a wholefood expert talk about the correlation between wholefoods and our bodies, is incredible. Don talks about how each different wholefood (that have been proven to assist towards health of different parts of our bodies), are in fact designed just like those body parts.

For example; A tomato is red and has chambers, just like our heart. We all know that tomatoes have been proven to be good for the heart. A walnut looks like a brain and it is proven that walnuts are great brain food. What does a celery stick look like? A bone. Guess what, celery is high in calcium and is good for our bones. These examples go on and on and it is mindboggling when you realise these simple, but effective correlations.

Now, there is an argument for diets that contain only wholefoods, but I personally have found that when I remove meats, (beef, chicken, fish) from my diet, I feel worse off. This is where it comes down to your own common sense and you knowing your own body. For most meals, I eat around 70% of vegetables and 30% of some kind of protein like beef, chicken, fish or pork. I eat more vegetables throughout the day, in homemade soups and I get around three serves of fruit through my own home-made smoothies; which contain no powders or chemicals.

My smoothies have whatever fruit is in season, but usually contain a banana, strawberries, blueberries, yoghurt and juice. Ok, so the juice is not

CREATE THE LIFE YOU WANT

100% natural, but it's pretty close. This smoothie is so tasty, so simple to make and I know is good for me; plus costs less than if I buy it, so it saves me money. My soups have a variety of vegetables, but for this, I do break my rule, by using liquid stock. This is the only time I use packet food that contain any traces of additives. The rest is all natural.

Manufacturers of prescription drugs and supplements won't tell you the truth about wholefoods, because there is no profit in whole foods for them. They hide behind fancy marketing plans and network marketing businesses and behind scare campaigns, through media and even your doctor. They understand that you are too busy to make a healthy meal, so they market you with a pill, powder or shake that saves you time, so you can spend more of your day on Facebook or Instagram.

The pharmaceutical industry has made a name for themselves, by attacking anyone who disagrees with them, or anyone who suggests that what the pharmaceutical industry is doing, is wrong. Thankfully, in recent years, there has been a move towards the public realising the extent of this scam by the pharmaceutical industry.

What the pharmaceutical industry also neglects to tell you, is the negative findings of the drugs and vitamins that they are selling you. By law they do have to publish all findings, but what you may not realise, is that these findings are hidden so deep in medical journals, that in most cases, hardly anyone has ever read them. As long as the manufacturers publish them somewhere, there are covered against liability.

Have you ever wondered why it is that only one-hundred years ago, there were somewhere in the vicinity of fifty diseases known to man, but these days, despite the thousands of anti-biotics and drugs that are available, we now have thousands of diseases? If you take the common-sense approach, it simply doesn't make sense, does it? How can we have so many drugs that are supposed to be making us healthier, yet we are sicker than we have ever been? It's simple. The pharmaceutical industry is a multi-billion-dollar industry and they have more power than any other industry, which they use to manipulate governments and mislead you into buying their products.

Health

I am not suggesting that all medicine is bad. There are some instances where they are required, particularly when it comes to trauma, but for the most part, the majority of drugs are doing the opposite, of what they claim to do. If the drugs they are designing were as good as they led us to believe, there would be no cancer, or any disease for that matter. The truth is, that it is simply not the case.

I recently saw an advertisement on television for a cold and flu medicine that was a prime example of how the pharmaceutical industry mislead the general public. The advertisement stated that the product had been "clinically *tested* to improve the severity of a cold". To most viewers, that would seem appealing, because they would immediately think that it is *proven* to reduce the severity of a cold. The key word here though, is "tested".

The ad didn't say that it was "clinically proven", it said "clinically tested". In other words, there were tests conducted, but no proof, that the product worked to reduce the severity of a cold. Based on this ad, I am certain that many people would have gone out and bought this product, thinking that it would greatly help, when in fact, it probably had little, or no effect at all on the severity of the cold.

I could go on and on about all of the cases where this type of misleading behaviour occurs in the pharmaceutical industry. I really just want to make the point, that if you want to be healthy, you need to cut the crap. Stop being misled and start to use the tried and tested approach, that has worked for thousands of years.

You don't need pills, powders or chemicals. All you need is good food. The secret to gaining the maximum nutrients from any food, is to eat it in a form, that is as close to its original source as possible. This means, fresh. Not tinned or processed (where possible). I do eat tinned tuna and occasionally have packet ham, but for the most part, I try to eat fresh foods. I eat crap food too like chips, ice-cream etc. but that's because I too get lazy and want my fix of junk from time to time. I try to limit them as much as I can, because I know that while they taste really good, they should be eaten in moderation.

CREATE THE LIFE YOU WANT

There is that word that we hear so often; moderation. We keep hearing it, because it really is the best way to stay healthy. I am all for having a drink occasionally, eating junk food sometimes and I certainly don't have a perfect diet. There is no such thing. If eat as much fruit and vegetables as possible, along with some lean meat and touch of the other food groups, then you will be well on your way to better health.

What is most important, is to stop stressing about having the perfect diet. Remember, stressing about that shit, will give you cancer, faster than what you actually eat, so eat well, but don't worry if you slip up once in a while. As I mentioned earlier, if you can create a body that is "alkaline", you will find that your energy levels are much higher than any amount of sugar, caffeine or artificial stimulant. The fastest way to get alkaline is to eat greens. Wheatgrass, spinach, broccoli, kale, cucumber and other greens are an easy way to be alkaline. If you can get a few serves of these every day, then you're well on your way to being healthy.

The most important lesson I want you to learn, is that you must question all that you read and hear when it comes to health. Don't just blindly take big corporation's word for it. I am not suggesting that you listen to "Doctor Google", but do your research and ask yourself the question; "Does it make sense"?

To me, what makes sense, is to eat a balanced diet, don't overindulge in junk, stop taking pills and powders and remove stress from my life. If what the pharmaceutical company is telling you doesn't make sense, they forget it. They want you to be fooled, because that is how they make money. If you're reliant on their product, then you will keep throwing your money away on it.

Not only are these pills and processed products not good for you, but when it comes to finance, this is the fastest way to being broke. I spend less each week by buying fresh foods and cooking all of my meals, than I would if I bought processed or packet foods and pills. I am not only saving my life, but I am saving a lot of money at the same time. You can do the same. It's not that hard. The only things stopping you, are the excuses you are telling yourself, as to why you're being so lazy.

Health

When I first finished working on cruise ships, I would eat seven fast food meals every week. That is at least one fast meal every day. The other meals would more often than not, be some kind of crap too, but as a minimum, I was eating KFC, McDonalds or Pizza every day.

When I first decided to eat healthier, it did take me some time to adjust and do it successfully, but when I look back, it really wasn't that hard. I was lucky that I lived with a chef when I first left school. He taught me that "anything goes" when it comes to cooking, so just experiment. That is what I did. Some things worked and others tasted like crap, but I learnt that it's not hard to eat healthy meals; for a small amount of money.

These days, I always cook enough dinner, so that I have left overs for lunch the following day. That way I am certain to have a healthy meal, rather than buy takeaway. When it came to ditching powders for smoothies, I went online and googled smoothie recipes, then went a bought a small blender and the ingredients that I wanted for my smoothies.

Another easy way to get lots of healthy vegetables, is to make soups. I love soup and I used to eat tinned soup a lot. Little did I know back then, that the soup I was eating, wasn't that healthy. Same as with the smoothies, I googled some soup recipes and started experimenting. I made the most awesome soups, with pretty much every vegetable known to man. I mix and match ingredients, depending on how cheap they are at the supermarket and I make enough to last me a week. A week's worth of soup will cost you less than $6, including the liquid stock and all the vegetables.

These are all easy to learn habits that anyone can do. I promise you, that within a few weeks of adopting this way of life, you will feel better, look better and have more energy. You will also save money, while creating an environment that disease simply can't survive in; all without a single pill or chemical. If you are suffering from ailments, there is a good chance, that these will also begin to subside, as the body starts to heal itself, just like it is designed to do.

I've long held the belief that our body is the product of our mind. This belief of mine came well before I discovered this truth, from Tony Robbins or Don Tolman. It has been said that what the mind can conceive, the body can achieve, so it makes sense that our mind controls how our body reacts to different situations.

I know personally, that when I used to get ready to go on stage for a show, I would never worry about my lines or choreography. I would simply trust my mind to guide my body; and it never let me down. If you want to be healthy, you must first see yourself to be that way in your mind.

If you combine that vision in your mind with good nutritional food, an active lifestyle and lots of water, sunshine and fresh air, your body will take care of the rest. If you want to learn more about how to live a healthy life through whole foods, I highly recommend Don Tolman's teachings. You can find out more at www.dontolmaninternational.com.

A few years ago, when I was settling into life after cruise ships, I was living with a couple of flatmates. One female I lived with confirmed everything that I believe to this, day about what I have told you so far in this chapter.

The female's name was Yolanda and she was roughly the same age as me. The house that we lived in, had a large kitchen, of which we designated different areas to each of the flatmates for food etc. One of Yolanda's areas, was a huge pot draw located under the kitchen bench. This draw was at least one metre wide and as deep as a typical kitchen bench.

In this huge pot draw, Yolanda had it filled to the brim with every vitamin, powder and dietary supplement known to man. The draw was filled to the top. Yolanda also had a water filter and distiller and all of her food, had to be organic. I would guess that if most people saw this, they would think, "She must be so healthy." Well, guess what?

She wasn't. Not only was Yolanda, not radiating health, she was constantly sick. She would average one sick day off work, every week, she was overweight and she always seemed to have some sort of cold-sore, infection or ailment. By the way, a cold, cold-sore or psoriasis, are your body's way of trying to get rid of something. These (and many other diseases), are your body's way of telling you, that something is wrong and that you need to put better things into your body.

To me, the reason that Yolanda was so unwell, was because her body had

Health

no immune system, as a result of her organic food and copious amounts of chemicals that she was putting into her body, by way of pills and powders. This may seem counter-intuitive, but I strongly believe, that we need some amount of resistance built up, from having "non-perfections" in our food. I am not suggesting that organic food is not good, but when combined with the amount of chemicals, Yolanda was putting in her body, her immune system, had nothing to fight with, to maintain its strength.

Yolanda's food and water were so "pure" that instead of her body having natural bacteria to fight with to maintain its strength, it was left vulnerable. This meant that any time she came in contact with a virus, her body was not able to fight it off.

In contrast to Yolanda, I drank tap water, ate non-organic foods and I took no pills or powders, yet I was never sick. Speaking of bottled water, while it may be convenient, unless you live in a third-world country, or a city where the tap water tastes disgusting, then stop wasting money on bottled water and get some natural grit into your body. Bottled water occasionally (like anything), won't hurt you, but if you religiously drink bottled water and nothing else, you are not only wasting your money, but you aren't doing your body any favours either.

I am lucky that where I live, the tap water tastes fine, so I rarely drink bottled water. If you need more proof that bottled water is one of the biggest scams these days, take a look at the name of one of the biggest and original bottled water manufacturers; Evian. If you spell the word "evian" backwards, you get "naïve". Isn't that ironic? Perhaps it is their message to us, as to how stupid they think we all are.

Another area that we've been misled, when it comes to health, is how much sunshine we should get. Several years ago, the A.M.A (Australian Medical Association) had a campaign stating that ten minutes in the sun, can be deadly. Obviously, excessive sun exposure is harmful to us and may lead to skin cancer, but this campaign was causing more ill-health, than it prevented.

By stating this misinformation, the AMA created a population in Australia, where 70% of Australian's were vitamin D deficient. It was only a few years ago, that the AMA retracted their statements and admitted that they were wrong. For us to get the required amount of vitamin D, we need to have exposure to the sun, for at least ten minutes per day, on at least our arms and face.

Anything less than this, can lead to vitamin D deficiency, which may lead to weaker bones and skeletal deformities. This is why I strongly recommend a healthy dose of sunshine, lots of water, fresh air and plenty of wholefoods, along with sufficient exercise, to maintain optimum health. Being healthy, really is that simple.

I hope that this chapter has opened your eyes to the truth and leads you to look further into the secrets of health and wellbeing.

Chapter Seven

Love

"Love is all you need."
—John Lennon

If there is one area of our lives that can swing from one extreme to the other; it is love and relationships. Love can create the highest of highs, or the lowest of lows. There is no doubt that when we're in love, as Belinda Carlisle sings, "Heaven is a place on earth". On the other hand, when it turns to custard, we end up with an "Achy breaky heart". Mastering this part of our lives can be the difference between happiness or misery.

The biggest mistake people make when it comes to love, is they believe that it can only come from an external source; in particular a person. Yes, human beings are wired to "relate" and that is where the word relationship comes from, but unless we start with ourselves, the rest of the picture will eventually fall apart.

It sounds like a cliché, but unless you love yourself, then it's not possible for someone else to truly love you. Many relationships, are based on two people entering into a love relationship, searching for something, to make them complete; instead of being complete already. By being complete when looking for love, we are able to give more of ourselves, because we are more whole. If we look for love when we don't fully love ourselves, then we end up settling for anything, just to be loved.

I make these statements, because I have done this myself. On many occasions, I have been desiring someone else's love and affection and therefore have foregone my own values, so that I am not alone. When I was in my twenties, I was a very social person and was always surrounded by people. After breaking up with my daughter's mother, I felt like I had to start looking for someone to settle down with and marry. I was only twenty-three, but I had this ideal, that society had suggested, that we all need to marry and have kids by a certain age, so I was on a mission.

As a result, I had to always be either in a relationship, or be hanging out with someone (mostly a female who I was attracted to). Very rarely was I alone. If I had a night off, or I was not doing anything, I would always call someone and arrange a date, so that I was not on my own. Subsequently, I bounced from one relationship to another. I dated all types of girls, who had some amazing qualities. Unfortunately, for the most part, they all had qualities that I didn't really like too.

Because I didn't want to be alone, I tolerated these qualities. That was until the point where I decided that the bad outweighed the good and the relationship ended. This was not to say that any of these girls were bad people; not at all. They were awesome girls, they just weren't right for me. Well, that's how I saw it at the time.

After a while, I realised that while I knew what I liked in a girl, I really didn't have an idea of what I really wanted. I knew that I wanted to be loved, but I wasn't sure of how to get it. Like most people, I had the attitude that I would know what I wanted, when it showed up in someone. The problem with this theory though, was that because I didn't know what I truly wanted, it didn't manifest into my life, because I was not sure when I saw it.

Like the law of attraction states, "what you focus on, becomes your reality". Because I wasn't focusing on any particular traits in women, I was being presented with all types of personalities and because I was just wanting to be loved, I would settle for whatever showed up. This was for fear of being left on the shelf, so to speak.

I've never had trouble meeting women and never had any problems finding women to go out with me, so I was hardly a desperate loser who couldn't get laid. I was just like a ball in a pinball machine; rebounding all over the place, until I got dunked down the exit chute. What I did know, was that like Johnny Lee wrote, I was "looking for love in all the wrong places".

Love

I did notice a pattern though, that the women I was attracting, were women who needing "fixing". I don't mean that they were any more messed up than anyone else, but, they all carried emotional baggage, from past relationships. By that stage, I had begun my journey of personal development, so I thought I knew enough, that I could help them. I had always been a giving person, so it felt like my job, to share what I had learnt with them, so they could be happy again. I guess, subconsciously, I thought that by "saving" them, they would be forever grateful and would want to stick around forever. How do you think that worked out for me?

What I didn't realise, was that not only was it not my job to help anyone, but the reason I was attracting them into my life, was because they were a mirror image of myself. Without realising, I too was like them and had some emotional baggage, from many years of emotional torment by my daughter's mother.

It wasn't until I saw an infomercial by Tony Robbins for his new audio program "Get the edge", that things began to change. At the time I was pretty broke, so the $204 Australian dollars that the program cost, was a big outlay for me. I had heard so much about this dude from the USA, that I thought "fuck it" and bought the program.

One of the first things Tony said on the relationship day was that "like attracts like." By this, he means that you will always attract people, who are similar to you, so far as your personality traits. This "ahha" moment, was long before I discovered the law of attraction, through the teachers of Esther and Jerry Hicks. The concept of like attracting like, is why you see so many couples who are similar in personality, looks or social stature together. You see a steroid filled body builder, with a muscle toned barbie doll, or you see famous celebrities together etc. You rarely see a smoking hot blonde goddess with a fat hairy dude. Well, maybe you do, but if so, I will guarantee that they are a mirror image of each other in a different way.

What I am saying and what Tony said, was that you will only ever attract someone like you. This is why I was attracting insecure women who had emotional baggage. At the time, I denied this was the case, but looking back, I can admit, that I had supressed these traits, because they were too hard to deal with.

As the famous US paster; Joel Osteen said, "Whatever is inside you will eventually show up on the outside." If you are an angry person, this is what you will attract; angry people. Have you ever wondered why someone keeps pushing your buttons or pissing you off? I can tell you without a shadow of a doubt, that the traits that you dislike in someone else, are the traits that you have not yet accepted in yourself.

This is a hard concept to grasp at first, and one that I too struggled with for a while. We all look at others and think, "there is no way I am like that." The truth is, that in some way, that same trait is inside us and that is why it annoys the fuck out of us. The key, is to look at a particular trait that you dislike in someone, and find where it appears in your life. This can be really tricky, but when you master it, life becomes much happier.

The great teachers such as Tony Robbins and Dr John Demartini teach this and while it is something that you may grapple with to start with, once you grasp the concept, your life will change. The only way to change the world, is to change yourself. You can't try to change everyone else in the world. You can't change every situation, but you can change you and the way you see the world. Once you change the way you see the world; your world changes.

When it comes to finding love, the starting point is never with someone else, it is always with you. I found this out when, after several years of back to back relationships, I decided to try a new tact. It was a year after my partner committed suicide. I had started dating again, but had encountered less than happy women or relationships.

I knew that this wasn't my fault, but it was my responsibility. Nothing in life, is your fault, but everything is your responsibility. With that in mind, I decided to take responsibility and take some time off from dating. I had some other things to deal with in my personal life, so I figured that it was a good opportunity to work on me.

As I focussed on me and my life without any distractions, the weeks and months went by. The longer the time went by, the more I began to feel at

Love

ease with being alone. From someone who was always wanting to be with someone, this was a strange feeling. I lived alone and was spending most of my time doing things on my own. The more I did this, the more I enjoyed it.

The more I found myself enjoying this time with myself, the more I realised, that I was no longer reliant on someone else to make me happy. Don't get me wrong, I would have still loved that intimacy, but I was no longer dependant on it, for my happiness.

This may not seem like a big deal, but what happened on a deeper level, was that I now viewed the "selection process" of dating someone much differently. No longer would I see a trait in someone that I may not particularly like and think, "that's ok, she has other good qualities" and date her anyway. In the past, I would have settled for things that I really despised, like someone being a smoker or being a stripper. There is nothing wrong with smokers or strippers, but for me, they are not things I want I a partner.

Just like someone may not like me, a 5/10 guy with blue eyes who doesn't do drugs or have a body full of tattoos, I am not into smokers or strippers and that is ok. Like I said, like attracts like, so you're going to attract like partners.

The first step to attracting your ideal partner, is to know what that ideal partner has, so far as personality traits and or looks. I've met many women, who have no clue what they want in a man and subsequently, never find it. How can you find something you're looking for, if you don't know what it is that you are looking for?

The reticular activating system in our brains, will go looking for the things that we want in our lives, once we decide what we actually want. Just like when you buy a brand new red car, you start seeing the exact same red cars everywhere. Once you know what you want in a partner, people with those traits will start to show up.

When I say, "what you want," I don't mean "hot blonde," "big breasts" etc. I mean, the qualities that you could not live without in a partner. As Tony says, the "must haves." The traits that, if your partner didn't have them, it would be a deal breaker. Everyone is different, so this list is going to be unique for you and that is how you will know when they come into your life. For example, if you must have someone who is honest, if you meet someone who is a compulsive liar, then that's not going to work.

While it's a good start to know what you want, I would suggest making a written list of these qualities. I'm not suggesting that you write the list and carry it on every date, but have it somewhere, so if you meet someone and have a few dates, you can then have a look, to see how many of "must haves", from your list, that they have.

Keep in mind, that getting to know someone, takes time, so while some traits may be obvious, others may take time to reveal themselves. Don't be too quick to rule someone out, if they don't tick all the boxes, right away. The key, is that your list can only have "must haves", not just "I would likes." While big breasts and lots of money, or tall, dark and handsome would be desirable, they are hardly going to be the main reason that a relationship lasts the test of time.

My list of must haves is quite long, but below, are a few examples of what I have on my list, so you have some ideas to get you started.

- Affectionate
- Willing to grow
- Nurturing
- Honest
- A lady
- Sincere
- Passionate

These are all traits that, if a partner did not have them, a relationship wouldn't last long with me. Remember, everyone's list is going to be different. If you're struggling to think of traits that a partner must have, then start with traits that you would hate them to have; then write down the exact opposite. I bet you can think of plenty of "no ways," in a partner.

Once you have your list, the next step, is to attract that person. The way you do that is by becoming the same person. Let me explain. If you want someone who is affectionate, but you hate any form of affection, they are more than likely not going to be attracted to you. This means that you must either have, or develop the traits that you desire in someone, in order to attract them.

You might be thinking, "why should I change for someone?" You don't have to change, but if you're wondering why you keep attracting the same traits that you despise, then perhaps this is an area you need to improve on in your own personality.

Like I said, nothing is your fault, but everything is your responsibility. To attract someone fit and healthy, you can't be a couch potato. It is unlikely to happen that way. Once you know what you must have in a partner, then you need to look at each trait and see how you can improve in that area. To some, this may seem like they must change, to suit someone. I don't see it that way. I see it as my opportunity to create a better me. If I become a better person, then I am the one benefiting, so why wouldn't I do it?

This leads me to a big reason why so many relationships fail. Many people go into a relationship, looking for W.I.I.F.M (what's in it for me). That is the number one reason why relationships fail. Tony Robbins summed it up perfectly when he said, "a relationship is a place that you go to *give*; not to *get*". Far too many relationships, are based on a mentality of, "I will do this, if they do that," instead of looking for what they can give their partner.

I was blessed to see firsthand, the incredible relationship that Tony and his wife, Sage have, when I attended his six-day "Date with Destiny" seminar in 2016. Tony and Sage have this amazing relationship, where they are always competing to see who can do more for the other. While most couples think, "I will do this, if they do that". Tony and Sage are the opposite. They are not focussed on what the other is giving them. They are focussed on how they can give more to their partner. This leads to an amazingly happy connection, where both people are totally fulfilled and their needs are completely taken care of.

The other difference with Tony and Sage, is that they don't need each other; they want each other. Each person is complete on their own, so they are not dependant on the other for their happiness. This is where self-love and self-esteem comes in.

When we are lacking in self-love or self-esteem, we tend to rely on others to prop that up. I see self-esteem as like a bank account and compounding interest. If someone gives you a compliment, it is like depositing a dollar into the account. That dollar is nice, but it is nowhere near as valuable as when you pay yourself a compliment. That dollar that someone else pays in, will be spent pretty quickly. On the other hand, if you pay yourself a compliment, that is like investing the dollar and receiving the benefits of compounding interest. It is much more valuable in the long term.

As was the case with my partner who committed suicide. I would always tell her how beautiful she was and how much I loved her, but she never told herself those things. Subsequently, when she was feeling depressed, she had no money in her self-esteem bank account, to draw on and make herself feel better. If you're relying on someone else to make you happy, you will never truly be happy. Happiness comes from within.

The thing that relationships do though, is they magnify emotions. A relationship, or friendship has the ability to make celebrations more magnificent and they also make burdens seem less daunting. When something awesome occurs in your life, it is great to celebrate it, but when you share that event with a partner, or friend, that feeling is magnified by sharing it with them.

On the flipside, if you've had a bad day at work, or have a problem you have to deal with, by sharing that issue with a partner, the problem is automatically halved by sharing it with them. That is the power of relationships, but first, you must find love within yourself, before you will be able to have it magnify in a relationship.

One other reason that I believe that many relationships fail, is because either the man or the woman (or perhaps both) are not in their natural energy. EG: masculine or feminine. In recent decades, there has been a "blurring" of energies. This began with feminists in the 1970's and has recently had a resurgence. Some women, have become more masculine in their core, because they feel that they must "compete" with men and men have become more feminine in their core as a way to please women.

There is much debate about how there should be "equality" in a relationship, however, as Tony explained, a successful relationship is not about equality, it is about polar opposites. While a relationship may work in the short term if both a man and woman are masculine in the energy, or both feminine, in the long term, it will only succeed, if there are polar opposites. In other words, one person must be in their masculine energy and the other in their feminine. Without sounding stereotypical or sexist, in almost every case, this must be the man in his masculine energy and the women, in her feminine energy. It's not that either sex can't have the opposite energy traits occasionally. It's simply that men and women are not designed that way.

This has nothing to do with equality and it doesn't mean that either sex is better or worse, than the other. They simply bring different things to a relationship. There will be times, where the man may take on more feminine energy and the woman more masculine energy, but for the most part, each person needs to remain in the own energy, at their core.

When I attended Date with destiny, of all the six days, the one that I thought that I would gain the least from, was day three; on relationships. I probably thought this, because, at the time, I was single, so I wasn't convinced that it would be relevant to me. I must admit, that this day, was by far the most powerful day of the entire event.

Throughout the day, Tony took us through various strategies and worked with couples around the room, while the rest of us watched, as he performed his interventions with the couples. Towards the end of the evening, Tony began talking about masculine and feminine energy and he discussed how these energies needed to be, for a relationship to work.

Tony discussed how in a relationship, there are three things that each partner must do, to nurture the relationship. For men there are the "Three – 'U's" that a woman must never feel. They are "Unseen, Unsafe and (not) Understood. Far too often, women feel unseen by their partner, the men don't truly understand their partner and they don't make their partner feel truly safe. A woman is at her most beautiful, when she feels safe enough to be completely vulnerable. This can only occur, when the man is not violating the "three – U's."

For a woman, they must make sure that they don't make the man feel the "Three – 'C's", which are Criticized, Closed and Controlled. Too often, women feel that they must criticize a man, to get him to do anything, they don't allow him to express himself, in his own way, or they make him feel like he is trapped. Tony explained that if a woman wants to know that a man will never leave, she needs to always make him feel like he is completely free. At first, this seems a little counter-intuitive, but upon reflection, it made perfect sense.

When a true man, feels like he has his freedom, he will never leave, because that is his nature, to protect his partner and family. Probably the one statement that stuck with me the most, during the event, was when Tony spoke in relation to how women can get the best out of their man. He said, "Nurture the boy (inside the man), and the man will show up". Tony was referring to the little boy that is inside every man, that needs to be nurtured. Every man wants to be the man, that his partner wants him to be.

It was then, that Tony began talking about a man's role in a relationship. Unlike, when talking about a woman's role, Tony didn't go into great detail, or explanation. Tony simply showed the audience, a five-minute clip, from Mel Gibson's movie; Braveheart. The scene was the part of the movie, where the men stood up and took back their freedom. When the video finished, Tony then asked the men in the room to stand. There were approximately 1,000 people attending, of which roughly half were men.

Tony stood on stage and said to the men in the room, that he wanted them to feel what it was like to be in their masculine energy. Tony then said, "I want you to make the sound, of what that means in your nervous system." Without another word said, Tony then yelled, "Freedom," as he punched the air, above his head. Suddenly, a massive roar of men yelling, "Yeah," filled the room. Once again, Tony yelled, "Freedom!" To which the men in the room, replied in the same way. This happened five more times, before Tony stood in silence for a moment, before once again yelling, "Freedom!" as the men replied by yelling, "Yeah!"

Tony then addressed the women in the audience. He said, "Ladies, look around the room, what do you see?" He continued, "There is not a man in this room, who is not completely centred or present. I didn't tell him to be centred or present, this is what men live to be, so that they can serve you

Love

and their family." As Tony asked the men to sit, the women in the room erupted into cheers and applause. Goosebumps covered my entire body and a sense of extreme pride filled my emotions.

Tony continued, "There wasn't one man who didn't tap into his core, when I uttered one fucking word". By this stage, the room was filled with so much energy. I myself felt the most masculine that I had ever felt in my life. Even though I was single, I felt like I was reacting on instinct, as if each of the women in the room, was my partner, my sister, my daughter or my mother.

When we discussed this, the following morning in our groups, before the day started, the women all said that in that moment, they felt so protected and safe, while the men felt so strong and felt so much love coming from the women in the room.

My point in telling this story, is that it is in our nature for men to be masculine in our core, and likewise, for women to be feminine in their core, for a relationship to work. If we stray too far from those energies, we are not fulfilled. It is essential that we have these polar opposites in a successful relationship. It is important for us to be conscious of whether or not we are in our own true core, when in a relationship.

I discovered on that day, that previously, I had been in my feminine energy too often in relationships, in order to please my partner. This is not to say that you shouldn't please your partner. In fact, when a man is in his masculine energy, he will naturally please his partner, because when he is in that energy, it comes naturally. Likewise, for a woman, when she is in her feminine energy, she will always let a man know that he has his freedom. Freedom is not something that a woman can take away from a man, it is something that a man gives to a woman.

When we can see these truths and realize that perhaps, we have all been going about relationships the wrong way, then everything gets a little easier and a whole lot more enjoyable.

Chapter Eight

Happiness

> *"Whatever is on the inside of you;*
> *will eventually show up on the outside."*
> —Joel Osteen

I said it earlier, but I want to reiterate it again. Whatever is inside of you, will show up on the outside. I have always thought of myself as a pretty happy person (like most of us do), yet up until recently, I always seemed to find myself attracting angry people. By that, I don't mean vicious people out to hurt me. I mean, people that seemed to want to disagree with me, or annoy me.

I've always understood that the traits we dislike in others, are in some way the traits that we've not yet accepted in ourselves, but I couldn't work out why I was facing these challenges. It was only a few months ago when I was preparing to write this book, that I was listening to an audio-book by televangelist; Joel Osteen and another, by Dr Wayne Dyer, when I began to understand what was happening.

Dr Dyer, who was one of the world's leading spiritual teachers, before his death in 2015, told a story about how, whatever was inside something, is what always comes out. He talked about how when you squeeze an orange, tomato juice doesn't come out; orange juice does. Why? Because that is what is inside an orange. When you squeeze a lemon; lemon juice comes out and so on. Even, when you squeeze a bull really tight, guess what comes out? A whole lot of bullshit!

Later that day, while listening to one of Joel Osteen's books, Joel men-

Happiness

tioned the quote, "Whatever is on the inside of you; will eventually come out." This is when it dawned on me, that if I was getting angry on the outside, and attracting angry people, then I must be angry on the inside. At that stage, I had not yet accepted that I was angry on the inside and that was exactly why I was attracting people into my life, who had the similar trait. These people kept showing up in my life, so that I could learn a valuable lesson.

Everyone that we attract into our lives, is a mirror image of ourselves. The universe, or god (depending on your beliefs) keep sending these people who hold a mirror up to us, so that we can see who we truly are. Once we see that, we have the power to change it; if we dislike what we see. If we don't see it, or deny it, then it keeps appearing in our lives, until we do see it and accept it.

This is essentially what the law of attraction is all about. Esther and Jerry Hicks are two wonderful spiritual teachers, who go so much deeper into this concept, than the movie "The Secret" ever did. They talk about how we "co-create" every single thing that shows up in our lives. There is nothing that happens by chance. Every situation and event, that is both good and bad, has somehow been created either by ourselves, or co-created with other people.

This is a very confronting concept and one that is hard to grasp at first, but if you can understand the truth in this, your life will change beyond belief. When I grasped that I was responsible for everything that showed up in my life, I was able to create only what I wanted and stop the things that I didn't want. While I am not perfect and I do still create some things that I don't much like, for the most part, I create a much better life, than I used to, prior to learning this several years ago.

By embracing this truth, you will be able to create the happiness in your life that you desire. You will no longer be waiting for a pay rise, a new partner, a new house or a better body to be happy. We often say, "I will believe it, when I see it", but as Wayne Dyer has often said, "You will only see it, when you believe it." If you're happy on the inside, this will lead to happiness on the outside. It will also put you in alignment with the universe so that you can attract all of the things that you desire.

This is the missing piece, that "The Secret" didn't tell you. They told you that all you have to do is ask for what you want and it will come. They said that to attract that which you want, you must be on the same frequency as the universe. What they didn't tell you though, is how to be on that frequency. I can tell you right now, that *the secret behind the secret; is to be happy.*

To be on the correct frequency to be able to attract your desires, you must be happy. That is the frequency. If you're not happy, then you're not going to attract what you want. If you're wanting a better body, because you don't like the one you have, you are not going to attract the better body, because you are making your requests from a place of lack and from an unhappy mindset.

You can't attract more money, by thinking about how little money you have. This is coming from a place of lack and will only result in you attracting more of what you already have; which is less money. To be in frequency and attract what you want, you must be happy with what you already have. If you are happy with that which you have, then this will allow more of the same to flow into your life.

Love the body you have, love the partner you have, love everything that you have and it will allow you to manifest the things that you really want. Whatever you are grateful for, will continue to show up in your life, so be grateful for the things that you do have, instead of complaining about what you don't have.

The Secret to Happiness

Having travelled to over 400 destinations around the world, I have been very lucky to have experienced so many different cultures and ways of life. I have been to rich countries, poor countries, third-world countries and communist ruled countries. What fascinated me most, was the different ways, they all lived.

Happiness

The first place that I started to notice this, was when I spent six months in Tahiti, working on a cruise ship. As an entertainer, I always had as much time on land as the passengers did, so myself and the other performers, would always explore the villages and beautiful islands.

Having grown up in Australia, I always had electricity, colour televisions, heating, internet and all the infrastructure that a developed country has. In French Polynesia (Tahiti) though, things were very different. People would ride around with ten people (including kids), in the back of a tray-back SUV style vehicle, cracking open bottles of beer on the side of the vehicle, as they drove along.

Their villages were basic, with most not having television, some only having basic electricity and none having proper internet. Their supermarkets were basic, in comparison to those back home. I was told that locals could eat any of the livestock (such as chickens or other animals) that roamed the streets; if they could catch it.

The locals didn't drink coffee, they had basic education and ate pretty basic meals as well. As a cast, we would often see these locals going about their lives and wonder what life would be like, if that was how we had to live. We often thought that if we found ourselves in that situation, that we would hate it. This made me feel sorry for these people. Little did I know, that perhaps, it was them who should be feeling sorry for me; not the other way around.

As my travels took me to more places around the world, I then realised, that the people who seemed to have the least in life, were the ones who appeared to be the happiest. They were people who had so little, yet they seemed so content. They didn't have half the possessions that I had, yet they were always smiling.

This made me realise two things. Firstly, that when we don't "compete" with others and when we stop comparing our lives to other people's lives, then we will be happy. These people simply didn't know that they didn't have internet. They simply didn't know any better and that made them happier. They weren't thinking, "people in Australian or America have internet, so our lives are not as good". They simply didn't know, so they didn't worry about it.

In developed countries, there is a destructive mindset, that says that we all need to compare ourselves with our peers, our friends or our neighbours. For some reason, we feel the need to have the latest phone, clothes, haircut and buy the biggest house, car and fake breasts, in order to feel better. All this does, is makes us unhappy. I am all for achieving in life, but my point here, is that if you're doing it for any other reason, than because it is *your* desire, then it can only lead to misery. If you're constantly competing with everyone to be better, you will find yourself feeling like a hamster on a spinning wheel, wondering, why the fuck you're not getting anywhere.

Secondly, seeing how the people in Tahiti lived, taught me that, in western civilisations, we tend to overcomplicate our lives. We fill our lives with all the things that we think will make our lives better, but all they do, is make it more stressful. Oprah Winfrey did a series of episodes on her show, where she sent "decluttering experts" into her fan's homes, to help them declutter.

On the surface, this seemed like just a superficial event, where the recipient could free up some space in their home. What it achieved on a deeper level, was each person who had their home decluttered, would have released a lot of tension, that was there from the feeling of being overwhelmed, with so much crap in their lives.

There is a direct correlation between the state of someone's home, car, office or life, to their level of stress and feeling overwhelmed. So many people hoard shit, in case they need it one day, but never use it. My mother of my ex (the ex who committed suicide), had so much crap in their house, that you could not walk in the front door, without bumping into something. The house was so full, that they had made a small path throughout the house so that you could walk from room to room. The house was wall to wall rubbish.

In my opinion, there was a direct correlation, between this mess and with the fact that her mother was severally obese and of ill health. To live in that environment, would not be good for anyone's emotional health.

Happiness

This is why Oprah was so invested in helping her fans, so that they could break through to create a better life.

I'm not suggesting that you have to live with nothing, or be a neat freak, but if your home is cluttered with rubbish and is a mess, it is going to affect your emotional state and therefore your productivity and even your level of happiness. The way to change this, is to declutter. Go through your house, wardrobe, garage and car and if you find anything that you have not used or worn in more than a year; get rid of it. Don't make excuses, just throw the shit out.

If you want to make this a really rewarding experience, then take everything that you don't need and donate it to a charity, so that it can change someone else's life at the same time. I do a declutter every few months and I love taking my stuff down to the local charity shop and giving it to the volunteers, because I know that someone who really appreciates it, will find it.

If you don't want to donate the stuff, then have a garage sale or sell it online. This will bring you quite a windfall and help to kickstart your investing journey, or help fund a holiday. You will be surprised how much money you can make selling old junk. As they say, "One man's trash, is another man's treasure."

When you declutter your life, you are also decluttering your mind. This will lead to an improved emotional state and overall happiness. Try it and see how powerful this is. The other thing this does, is that on an emotional and spiritual level, it frees up your life to receive new things. It may sound strange to some, but I can assure you that on so many occasions, when I have given things away, new things that I have desired, have suddenly manifested in my life.

If the Tahitians can live a simplified life, so can you. I have everything I need, but I don't have endless amounts of crap from ten years ago, that I only keep for sentimental reasons. Once you simplify your life, you will begin to see the true meaning of happiness.

Happiness isn't a place you arrive; it's a state of mind, a decision and a way of life. Happiness is not something that you gain; it is something that

CREATE THE LIFE YOU WANT

you choose. I used to think that when I get the pay rise, the new car, or the hot girlfriend, that I would then be happy. When I arrived at those places, I felt happy for a moment, but that didn't last.

Being happy comes from within; not from external things, events or people. Yes, these things can make you feel good for a moment, or a while, but unless you make happiness something that you choose every day, they will fade out at some point and you will be left feeling unhappy.

The fastest path to happiness, is through gratitude. You can't be grateful and sad at the same time. The more you are grateful, the more you will be happy. We all seem to think that in order to be happy, we need to have a grand purpose in life, or a spectacular job and if we don't have that grand purpose, that we're not important and therefore not happy.

The key to happiness is finding what your purpose is and live it, whatever that is. Find what you love, then find a way to do it and even make a living from it and you will find happiness. This could be the smallest of thing, or the most insignificant job or purpose to others, but if it is special to you, then it is your purpose.

I spent the first ten years of my working life, doing what I thought I was supposed to do. The things that society suggested that I did, like have a secure job, be responsible, etc. I found myself at twenty-three, giving up my dream of being a recording artist and instead working full-time in the hospitality industry. I was good at my job, yet I was so unhappy. I had the security of the job, yet I was unfulfilled.

A few months later, I was an unexpected father and even more so, I felt compelled to continue on this path, in order to be a good father and partner, by providing for my young family. It was only after the following six years of torment by my partner (who was by that stage, my ex-partner), that I finally decided that I was not willing to settle for this life.

A series of events led me to auditioning for cruise ships and I spent the following ten years working at sea as the lead male vocalist performing in Broadway shows at sea. I was living my dream and was doing what many people dreamed of doing; being paid to do what I loved while travelling the world.

Happiness

This life isn't for everyone. Even though in my eyes, it was perfect, to some, it may not be so wonderful, because it would mean that they would have to spend six months at a time being away from their loved ones. This was my purpose at the time. Yours will be different, because you are different.

Don't try to live someone else's dreams. Find what it is that you desire and not those of what looks good, or that society dictates you should do. My ultimate life is no longer being at sea all the time, but I am certainly not perusing a "normal" life either. I now love writing and being creative in different ways to how I used to.

Writing books, screen plays and being creative is the direction that I am headed. Your dream may change too, so don't be disappointed if it is short lived like mine was at sea. "You don't have to change the world; just don't fuck it up for the next generation," was a great quote that I read and one that I like to live by. My purpose isn't to be the world's greatest anything; other than the world's greatest version of me. My purpose is to do what I love and do it to the best of my ability; that is what makes me happy.

An example of this is the way that I choose to give to those in need. I learnt from Tony Robbins and many others, that giving provides the giver tremendous joy. Tony feeds millions of people every year and while I would like to do this, I simply cannot at this stage.

What I did learn from Tony, was that we can all do something, however small, to give to those less fortunate than us. There is an organisation where I live, that sets up a van near the beach, for homeless people to come and have a cup of coffee and a chat in the evenings. I decided to go and buy some inexpensive gifts and wrap them at Christmas and take them to this spot to give them out. They were $5 each and all up, cost me less than $100, but I know that it would have brought some joy to the people who received them.

I also grew more than twenty herb pots filled with Basil, which I wrapped for Christmas and delivered to the shop, that the volunteers for this charity work from. This was my gift to the volunteers who spent their hours helping these homeless people. They give so tirelessly for others, so I wanted to say thank you to them.

The thing about these types of gestures, is that while it brings joy to others, I can tell you, that I get so much more out of it, by doing it. The joy I get from knowing that in some small way, I have contributed to someone, is the best feeling.

I recently served a year probation after my incident that led me to being imprisoned for ten days, so I was unable to leave the country during that time. For someone who has travelled so extensively, this was tough. When I was finally able to travel, I did. I had a plane ticket booked for the day after I was free to go. When I was booking the trip a few months earlier, I didn't care where I went, as long as I could get away.

I decided to go to Bali for five days to relax. I had been to Bali twice before, so I only wanted a short trip to escape. As I was arranging the trip, I remembered that there was an orphanage in Bali, that many travel agent friends had visited. I made contact with one of them, who gave me the details, so I could contact the orphanage. I did some research and discovered that they required children's clothes for the orphans.

I knew that I was only going for five days and in Bali, I really only wear shorts and t-shirts, both day and night. This meant that while I had 23kg of possible luggage, I would have lots of room in my suitcase for kid's clothes. Having been in the travel industry, I contacted Virgin Australia, who I was flying with and asked them for an allowance to take an additional suitcase.

Virgin Australia were so good and allowed me an additional 23kg to take. This gave me a total of 46kg that I could take with me. I spent the next few months asking anyone I knew, to donate unwanted clothes, that I could give to the kids in Bali. I also went and bought hand sanitiser and toiletries that the orphanage needed. I ended up with two full suitcases weighing 46kg in total, of which 5kg was for me.

I spent a few days relaxing in Bali and arranged for a local driver to take me to the orphanage which was located an hour away in the mountains. We arrived at the orphanage and I was greeted by a group of children, aged from three to fourteen. They were all the friendliest and most loveable

Happiness

children I had ever met. The organiser took my suitcases full of gifts, while I spent time playing games with the children and exploring the orphanage.

This orphanage is one that specialises in medical and dental needs for orphans, with special requirements. Despite these kids challenges in life, they were all so happy. One little boy who was three, had legions all over his scalp and was constantly receiving medical treatment, yet he was so happy and playful.

I met a beautiful young lady who was fourteen. She was the oldest there and informed me that she wanted to be a doctor when she was older. This was a classic example of how the love and compassion of others had influenced her to do the same one day. She was the most beautiful soul and she had a wisdom far beyond her age.

I spent an hour or so there and when I left, I felt so full of love and joy for these kids. I had given them a gift, that would enhance their lives, but that paled in comparison, to the gift that they had given me, through our encounter. These are the types of things that bring happiness to life. Experiencing the joy of giving to another, no matter how big or small.

If you have the opportunity to do something similar, I urge you to do so. The experience will change your life. It will give you such a beautiful perspective and make your heart sing. If you are travelling to Bali and want to donate to the same orphanage, as I did, you can visit their website www.balikids.org where you will find the latest updates of what clothes and supplies they currently require for the kids.

There are several "orphanages" in Bali, however, many of them are not actually orphanages. They are a front for dodgy companies. They even go as far as having people drop their kids off at the premises during the day, to create the appearance of being an orphanage, so please do your research, if you wish to donate to any other orphanage, other than Bali Kids. I know firsthand the great work that Bali Kids do, hence why I recommend this one.

You don't have to physically take your donations up into the orphanage. There are various drop off points in Bali, that you can leave them, to be collected. You can also make donations of money if you wish. All the details are on their website.

Because I have travelled to 400 destinations around the world, when I travel these days, I try to do little things like this. This means that I get to experience a destination and leave my small mark on the lives of those I meet. It may not be grand, but it is special. Is there some way that you can do something similar? I am sure there is. You don't have to do like I do, or do like Tony Robbins does. You can find your own way to give something back and I am sure that when you do, you will be rewarded in ways you could have never imagined.

What My Dogs Taught Me about Happiness

"If you can't eat it or fuck it; then piss on it and walk away"—Bailey and Bella (My dogs)

I think that the above quote, by my dogs, is by far the most useful quote that I have read. We get so caught up in our lives and let things get so overcomplicated, that we often forget to enjoy life and be happy. I have two of the funniest kelpie dogs that I have ever met. They embrace life (as most dogs do), in a way that we all should.

The way I ended up with two dogs, seemed at the time to be by chance, and perhaps a burden, but as time went on, I realised that it was divine timing when they appeared in my life. My dogs arrived less than a year before I was wrongly imprisoned. This was just enough time for the three of us to bond in a way, that now, I would give up anything, to have them in my life.

It is often said that dogs are man's best friend. I for one, didn't truly grasp that concept until these two dogs were literally all that I had in life. When I was released from prison, I had no job, no money, quite a bit of debt, all of my family, (except for one brother) had deserted me and I had lost every single one of my friends, as a result of the misleading media

Happiness

reports. I probably would have deserted someone too, if I was gullible enough when reading those things about someone.

There I was. I had a roof over my head, (just), a few hundred dollars and my two dogs. Somehow though, for the first time in my life, I was actually happy. Don't get me wrong, I was stressing about how the hell I was going to survive, with no job and I was pretty disappointed in having lost so many (what turned out to be fake) friends, but I was at peace.

I sat on the lounge, watching TV playing with my dogs, when I realised how much we can learn from them. Have you ever noticed that when you come home, dogs are so ecstatic to see you; even if you only went out to the letterbox? Dogs have such an amazing energy for life. They run, jump, play and do everything at full pace every single day, until they can't go any further. Then they rest. Their zest for life is something that I try to emulate myself.

The other thing dogs have, is unconditional love. You can yell at a dog and they still love you, whereas, if you look sideways at a human, you are public enemy number one. I think the human race should be more like dogs and love each other unconditionally, regardless of race, religion or whatever else we are emotionally fighting each other about.

The thing I admire most about my dogs (and all dogs), is that when it comes to problems, they have a simplistic approach to every problem. Dogs look at something, size it up and if they can't eat it, or fuck it, they piss on it and walk away. Why can't we look at our problems that way? We get so emotionally invested in outcomes and problems that we overcomplicate them and make them seem worse than they are.

I try to be like my dogs. I look at a problem and like them, if I can't eat it, or fuck it, I figuratively piss on it and walk away; without giving it a second thought. Apart from the before mentioned traits that I love about dogs, the three things that I think we should all learn from dogs are to be curious, be playful and to explore.

Let's look at these individually.

Be Curious: Dogs are always curious. They may not speak, but they are always curious about new things and new experiences. As humans, we tend to get so set in our ways, that we stop growing. We hate change and we don't like anything that is different.

I learnt at the age of twenty, when the five-star international hotel that I was working for, was bought out by one of the largest chains in the world; Accor Hotels. The first morning that Accor took over, we were brought into a meeting and told that there would be lots of changes. Our new General Manager; Buddy Byrd (yes, that was his name), told us that we needed to embrace change. At the time, I didn't think too much of it, but as it turned out, this has led to some of my greatest achievements in life.

These days, if things aren't constantly changing and evolving, then I get bored. I love change. When changes occur, is when we grow the most. Don't get set in your ways. Embrace change and go looking for it. Change is the spice of life and the key to exponential growth.

Be playful: Dogs are always so playful. No matter how exhausted my two dogs are, they are always up for play time. They run around and have such fun, all day. Wouldn't be nice if we too could be like that? Life wasn't meant to be a chore. Sure, we need to do certain things to survive in society, but why can't we add an element of playfulness to everything we do?

From a young age, I was always the class clown. When someone said, "Hey wouldn't it be cool if someone did this," I was the kid who actually did it. I was not very popular with teachers most of the time, but my school friends, knew they could count on me for a laugh. To this day, I enjoy that role. Even if there is no one around, I often find myself doing stupid things to make myself laugh.

A trick I learnt from Tony Robbins, was to be able to change my state at any moment. If you're feeling down, or upset, the fastest way to turn it around it to change your state. This can be done with music, exercise, or as I do, by doing something stupid. This may be for me to pull a funny face, slap myself across the face, fart, or anything that will break the pattern that I am in at the time.

What this does is it interrupts my current pattern, so that I can change it and make a new one. Tony is a master at pattern interrupting. If you have seen his documentary on Netflix; "I am not your guru," or attended any of his events, you would have seen how he interrupts someone's pattern, which is the first step to creating change, in someone's life.

This is where being playful (which I learnt from my dogs), is important. By being playful, you rarely find yourself being caught up in negative behaviour, and if you do, you can easily change your state, by being playful and therefore drag yourself out of almost any rut you may find yourself in; instantly. This is not to say that you treat life flippantly. It simply means that you don't take life too seriously, or spend too much time being bogged down by negative emotions. As Ferris Bueller says, "Life moves pretty fast. If you don't stop and look around once in a while; you could miss it."

Explore: The final thing that I have learnt from my dogs, is to explore. Have you ever noticed that dogs are always looking for new things to sniff and new places to explore? They find every situation, place and new experience, so fascinating. Like me, my dogs, don't like the same old mundane experience. They get bored and start to show destructive behaviour, such as barking and digging, if they aren't stimulated.

If you're feeling "stuck" in life, then perhaps it's because you have made your life too regimented. I agree that structure is important and so is discipline, but make sure that you don't settle for a "comfort zone". That is the quickest way to achieving nothing.

Speaking of comfort zones, in one of the first books I read, by Paul Hanna, he explained that our comfort zone works just like an autopilot in a plane. Just like the plane, we set our altitude to a certain range and if something happens in our life, that takes us out of our comfort zone, our "auto-pilot" brings us back to that comfortable place. You may be thinking, "that doesn't sound too bad," but let me explain.

The auto-pilot of a plane is set so that if the plane drops below a desired altitude, the auto-pilot automatically brings the plane higher so that it is back in the "comfort zone". The same applies if the plane is flying too high.

Our comfort zone is the same. If something dreadful happens in our life, which drags our self-esteem or happiness down, our auto-pilot automatically lifts us back up to where we feel comfortable. Have you ever noticed that humans tend to bounce back from adversity well? That is why. Unfortunately, the same occurs when something great happens in our life. When something awesome happens that makes us feel really good, our auto-pilot says, "Hang on. This isn't normal. I have to make an adjustment." Then we find ourselves back in that comfort zone.

You may be thinking, "Why would anyone want to do that"? Well, I doubt that anyone wants to do that, but none the less, because our subconscious controls more of our actions than we realize, more often than not, we have no choice and don't realise it is happening.

This is referred to as "self-sabotage." Humans are generally wired so that life stays on a reasonably level playing field. We like it when nothing too bad happens, and subconsciously, nothing too bad happens either. As its been stated many times, more than 95% of our thinking is done subconsciously. In other words, unless we consciously think about what we are thinking about, then we are not really thinking about it. As Christopher Howard says, "You can't not think about what you're thinking about, without thinking about it". Confused?

The key is to identify when you are subconsciously sabotaging your life. The way to do this, is to firstly, raise your standards to take yourself out of your comfort zone, then make that your new comfort zone. If you continue to take yourself out of your comfort zone (raise your standards), then what happens, is being outside of your comfort zone, becomes the new "comfort zone." The way to achieve this, is to be like my dogs, and explore and keep exploring.

Having read over 280 books, I have had the pleasure of hearing some of the greatest stories ever told. All of the 280 books, that I have read, have been non-fiction. In particular, the topics have all been on some form of personal development / self-improvement. The authors that I have studied, all have a unique style and something special to bring to their readers. One particularly gifted author and speaker; is Dr Wayne Dyer.

In one of his books, Dr Wayne Dyer gives a wonderful example of how

Happiness

life should be lived, by using the old children's nursery-rhyme, "Row, row, row your boat". I'm not sure if this is something that he came up with himself (highly possible), or if he himself was relaying it. Either way, I want to share this story with you. It really does explain, how to live a happy life.

The first verse of the song, which we all know so well, goes like this:

"Row, row, row your boat, gently down the stream"
"Merrily, merrily, merrily, merrily, life is but a dream"

If we take the lyrics and break them down, there are some clues, as to how to live a happy life.

"Row, row, row *your* boat" – The song doesn't say "row someone else's boat". It says row "*your boat*". Stop trying to live your life on someone else's terms, or the way that they live theirs. Do what you want to do and live how you were meant to live.

"*Gently*" – There is no mention in the song, of rowing your boat forcefully or aggressively. Row your boat "gently" and peacefully. There is no rush. There is no finish line in life. We are all living on different time frames, so if someone gets a pay rise before you, buys a house that's bigger than yours, or gets a better body faster; that's ok. There is no need to compete with people who are running different races. It's like having a scientist and a body builder compare themselves to each other. You are rowing your own boat, at your own pace.

"*Down* the stream" – I personally couldn't think of anything more stupid, than trying to row up stream and wondering why I am getting nowhere. As Tony Robbins says, "It's like running east, looking for a sunset. No matter how fast you run, it is not going to happen." Life is not meant to be so hard. If you believe that it is, then that is why it is. Let the river of life take you to where you are meant to go. Yes, you can negotiate obstacles along the way, but stop trying to battle against the currents. Go with the flow.

"*Merrily, merrily, merrily, merrily*" – Most importantly, enjoy the ride. Embrace every moment. Be grateful for everything that you experience. The more grateful you are, the more things to be grateful for, that will show up. When you're happy, happy things, events and people present themselves to you.

Finally; *"Life is but a dream"* – Everything that is in your external world, began in your internal world. Everything that you have in your life, is a result of what was once just a dream. Dream big and dream often. Dream of everything that you desire, then watch those dreams manifest into reality, (with a little decision making and action taking, of course).

You may not realise it, but you and I and everyone on earth, have the power to create anything. I have never been a person who would refer to myself as religious, but when I recently read a book called "Conversations with God," by Neale Donald Walsch, it finally dawned on me that we are all divine beings. Before I get into the detail, I want to make the point that I am using the word "God" as a way to refer to our creator. There is so much disagreement about religion in the world, over who has the best God or higher source. I am not saying that this story belongs to Christianity or any other religion.

I am not here to state any case, or dispute any beliefs. In my honest opinion, I believe that while each religion may call it something different, essentially, we all believe in the same thing and all pray to the same God. We just call them something different; depending on our religious beliefs. For the purposes of this story, I will use "God", but please know, that this applies to whatever higher source, that you pray to, or believe in.

Conversations with God is a transcript of conversations that Neale had with God, over a series of nights. At first, the dialogue could be seen as a bit staged, for anyone who is not a true believer in God, or a human's ability to interact with the lord. As you read on though, you can't help but be drawn into acceptance of what is occurring. The questions that Neale asks, are the questions that we all have, when it comes to god, prayer and how we should go about it. What is special, is the form that the replies from God came to him.

The version I read was the audio book, so it was even more authentic, given the casting of the voices of God. The voice of God alternated between a male and female voice, narrated by Edward Anser (of Mary Tyler

Happiness

Moore fame) and Oscar and Tony award winning actress; Ellen Burstyn. The book is so brilliantly written and Neale is so candid throughout, that you can't help but accept all of its insights; no matter how farfetched you first thought they were.

Throughout the book, there is an underlying question of who God is. As the book comes to its conclusion, it is revealed that God is in everything and in fact; in everyone. Who is god? I am god. You are god and everyone is god. God is everything that we are and we are everything that God is.

There is no right, no wrong, no good, no bad. Everything just is. Everything is precisely how it is meant to be and everything is part of the grand master plan. God created us and everything around us, so if we are God, then doesn't it make sense that we have the same power to create anything in our lives?

There is nothing that you cannot be, do or have in life. We are all created in the image of God, so why not create magnificence; like God does. There is a misconception that heaven is a place that we go to if we are good, but heaven is actually here on earth. We are constantly surrounded by god and angels; as well as the "devil." We often think of ourselves being humans, having a spiritual experience, but the truth is, that we are spiritual beings, having a human experience.

When it comes to spiritual enlightenment, there some amazing teachers and authors. In my opinion, there are a couple who really stand out. Ether and Jerry Hicks and Dr Wayne Dyer. Of all the spiritual type books that I have read, the above-mentioned authors take up most of my list on this topic.

When I began reading these types of books ten years ago, I first found Esther and Jerry and then noticed that Dr Dyer had provided the foreword to one of their books, so I decided to explore his teachings; and I am so glad I did. I urge you to see where your reading leads you in the same way. Many of these great teachers work together, admire each other and many of their lessons flow into one another.

I have a list of books that I recommend at the end of this chapter, but

CREATE THE LIFE YOU WANT

I wanted to make special mention, of these two authors in particular, as they are in a class of their own.

Below is a list of incredible spiritual / enlightenment books that I highly recommend.

Dr Wayne Dyer:

- *Being in Balance*
- *Divine Love*
- *Excuses Begone*
- *Secrets of an Inspirational Life*
- *Manifest Your Destiny*
- *Choosing Your Own Greatness*
- *Your Sacred Self*

Esther and Jerry Hicks:

- *Ask and It Is Given (Part 1 & 2)*
- *The Law of Attraction*
- *The Teachings of Abraham*
- *Living the Art of Allowing*
- *Finding the Path to Joy*
- *The Vortex*

There are so many more great books by these authors, as well as by Susan Jeffers, John Demartini, Joe Vitale, Eckhart Tolle, Deepak Chopra, Marianne Williamson, Joyce Mayer, Bob Proctor and many more.

Probably my favourite book in this genre though, is *The Alchemist*, by Paulo Coelho. The book is a wonderful spiritual teaching, written in the form of children's fable. It tells the story of a young shepherd boy, named Santiago, who goes on a search for worldly treasure. He meets various people along the way, as he encounters a series of lessons. While he travels great distances to find these treasures, he discovers that those treasures are

Happiness

much closer to home than he first thought. Along the way, he discovers his "personal legend" in life.

It's a fantastic book and one that every reader will gain a different inspiration from. I won't give too much away here, but I urge you to take a look at this incredible tale. The book is quite short and even as a not so good reader, I was so captivated by it, that I read the paperback version is less than twenty-four hours.

The one thing that this book, along with many other books taught me, was that my journey was different to that of anyone else and that I must follow it, instead of someone else's. Too often in life, we take on someone else's dreams or goals that society have subconsciously placed on us. We are all unique and no one has the exact same desires inside them. We may have similar desires, but often, these are as a result of societal influences and not those that emanate from our heart.

Not everything that shows up in your life is your fault, but everything in your life is your responsibility. Everything currently in your life, is a result of an action or a thought that you have made. This will take practise to accept and get used to, but when you do, your life will change dramatically.

Don't be swayed by others influences or the media or anyone telling you what you should focus on. The media are a disgraceful industry that thrive on fear and hatred for their success. Terrorisms is so rife in the world, because of the way the media fuel it. The media's sole intention is to create emotion. This is what leads to readers and clicks on their websites, which is how they sell advertisement spaces.

The media want you to focus on war, terrorism and hatred, so they can keep control of their own agendas. Thankfully, in recent years, there have been some great teachers such as Wayne Dyer, plus Esther and Jerry Hicks, who have enabled a shift in consciousness. This is growing and slowing gaining momentum. If you want to reduce war, you don't focus on it. Or "fight against" it. That only adds more fuel to it and allows it to grow.

If you've ever watched a fire burn, it needs three things to survive; fuel, oxygen and heat. If you take one or more of these three things away, the fire goes out. Terrorism, domestic violence and war are the same.

CREATE THE LIFE YOU WANT

We have this horrible situation in Australia at the moment where there is so much focus on domestic violence. Yes, there is too much domestic violence in Australia and everywhere, but the problem is, that the media have manipulated so many people into thinking that the way to stop domestic violence is to "fight against domestic violence." That is the most ridiculous thing I have ever heard.

"Anything we fight, will only get stronger." —John J Murphy

Mother Teresa was once asked if she would "join in a 'march against war,'" to which she said, "No, but if you have a march for peace, I will join that." This is precisely the mindset that we need to adopt, if we want to stop domestic violence, war, terrorism and anything else that we want to stop.

Pushing against something, is only going to create more of it. When you push against someone, they push back and neither one moves. If you have a fire, you don't add fuel to it, unless you want it to get bigger. Adding hate, anger and "fight" to terrorism, war, or domestic violence, is only going to make it a bigger problem. That is exactly what is happening in Australia at the moment. In the last three years since the "fight against domestic violence" started, the number of domestic violence incidents in Australia has increased; not decreased.

As a result of the increase, media outlets and many people are saying that they need to "continue the fight." It baffles me, how we can firstly be so naive to the media's manipulation, but also, how we could think that creating more anger and hate, would be the answer. As a result of the "fight", much more anger towards men has led to more provocation by women and more reaction by men, which has led to more violence.

I am not suggesting for a moment, that there is any justification for any form of violence, but the way the media has manipulated the public, it has created a "blame game" effect where now we have women (and men) thinking that they can antagonise their partner and if they do and their partner reacts, it is in no way their fault at all.

War and domestic violence, or violence of any kind, rarely happens as a result of just one person or one side. Just like fire not being able to survive

Happiness

without fuel, neither can violence. At the moment, we are adding fuel to violence, instead of taking it away. The only thing that will stop domestic violence or war; is love. It can't survive if we take away the heat or the fuel.

This goes back to my earlier comment about nothing being your fault, but everything being your responsibility. We are all responsible for everything that is in our lives right now. One of the greatest teachings I have learnt, was from Esther and Jerry Hicks, by way of "co-creating." Despite what I have just said about focussing on these things that are perceived as bad, the world always has and always will be in perfect balance.

When studying Esther and Jerry Hicks, along with Dr John Demartini and Dr Wayne Dyer, I discovered what few people know. That is, that everything is exactly how it should be. For most people, it is a really hard concept to grasp, because they see people starving around the world, countries at war, so much hate and anger, as well as racism and an earth that is said to be disintegrating.

These things are certainly true for those who look for these things and focus on them and while I am not suggesting that they are not happening, I see the opposite. This is where the world is in perfect balance, as Dr Demartini suggests. For every act of hate, comes an act of love, for every starving person, someone is giving their time, money and resources to help. For every environmental issue, there are people striving for ways to fix them.

As hard as it may be to accept that the world needs things that we perceive as bad, this is the way it needs to be. As Isaac Newton said, "For every action, there is an equal and opposite reaction". What happened immediately after the world trade centre buildings were brought down in what has been described as the worst terrorist attack in history? The entire world, displayed tremendous love and compassion for each other. New Yorkers, who were traditional known as cold people, were suddenly so much warmer and friendlier. The pregnancy rate and subsequent birth rate, in New York, in the following months after 9/11 increased dramatically.

As terrible as this event may have been to people, without the event, these other things would not have occurred. I am not suggesting that in order to love, you always have to go through death, but the universe ensures that if the world becomes out of balance, it is brought back into balance; very quickly.

Have you ever noticed that if you receive an unexpected windfall, such as a bonus pay at work, or you find fifty dollars, that almost immediately a bill shows up? There have been so many documented cases of this and I myself, have noticed it on many occasions, in my own life. When I was working in the travel industry, I made a huge mistake in booking a client's airfares, which lead to me wearing a $522 loss in commission for that month. No sooner had I fixed the problem and accepted the loss, a gentleman called and booked a business class flight from Australia to London, in which the airline paid me exactly $522 in commission.

If you look, these types of things are happening everywhere, every day. People get so angry about global-warming, the great barrier reef being destroyed and many other so called "imbalances" in the world. I never worry about them, because I know that for every person protesting trees being cut down, there are just as many people planting tress somewhere else. Plus, for the most part, it is mostly media hype and very little truth in what we are being told.

I have no problem with people protesting things, even though I never do, because I know that if we all protested something, then that would put the world out of balance. The world needs all types and we all have a purpose on earth, even murderers, rapists and criminals are an essential part of keeping the world in balance.

Don't get me wrong, I am not condoning these crimes at all and my heart goes out to those who have suffered from such crimes, but that is precisely my point. As dreadful as we see these crimes as being, each one teaches us to be compassionate, empathetic, loving or caring.

The world and all of us in it, need to understand that polar opposites are required in life. While we would all like only wonderful things in our lives, we must understand and embrace the fact that we will always have an opposite for everything in life.

You cannot know what pleasure feels like, unless you've experienced

Happiness

pain. To know love; you must first understand hate. In order to feel joy; you must first know sadness. In order to feel wealth; you must first know poverty. For without each duality, we can't know it's opposite.

We need to realize, that it is only through understanding and experiencing what we perceive as bad, that we can know what good is. Having said that, there is literally nothing in this world that is either good, or bad. There is only what we perceive something to be. The same event experienced by two people, can have vastly different meanings, based purely on the meaning that they each give the event.

Two brothers who were subject to an abusive father as children, could turn out very differently. This type of situation has been documented and spoken about many times, where one son grows up angry, violent and hating his father. He spirals into drug abuse and alcoholism, where as his brother, goes through life with such compassion and love. These two brothers had the same experience, yet they had very different responses to it.

True happiness comes from being able to embrace all that life has to offer and knowing that nothing has any meaning, other than the meaning that we give it. Instead of thinking that there is good and bad, realise that things just are. If something happens in your life, that you perceive as bad, look for what it is that you are being taught is good about that event.

We go through life thinking that we must make everything good and not have anything bad in life. Some motivational speakers teach you that you must think positively. This just leads to disappointment in the end. Tony Robbins, who most people think is the "Mr positivity" motivational speaker, is in fact not as much this way inclined, as most think. Tony is certainly not about negativity, but he teaches that you can't create the live you want, by simply thinking positively.

We all have negative thoughts, and as Tony teaches, we can learn from these thoughts. It's great to have a positive attitude, and I am more positive than negative, that's for sure. As Tony suggests though, we need to stand guard at the door to our mind and control our thoughts, otherwise, our thoughts will control us.

As Tony says, "Either you master your mind; or your mind masters you." If you want a spectacular garden in your home, you don't look at it and say, "There are no weeds, there are no weeds, there are no weeds." You look at the garden, see the weeds, then rip them out. It is only by standing guard at the door of your mind and monitoring your thoughts, that you can weed out the negative ones and replace them with better thoughts. Accept that negative thoughts are a sign, to take action in some way or another.

This may sound a little contradictory, but let me explain. You are going to have negative thoughts sometime. What Tony is saying and what I am suggesting, is that you identify them as negative, see how they can affect you and replace them with a more productive thought. Negative thoughts can also be a great sign that you need to take action in some part of your life.

You may look in the mirror and think, "geez, I'm fat." That on its own, is not a great place to be emotionally, but not thinking it at all, is not going to help either. You can't just say, "I am super skinny and healthy," if you are overweight. What your negative thought is telling you, is that you need to take action. You may see yourself as fat, but if you find yourself thinking that, then stop the thought immediately, replace it with a thought such as, "I am going to get fit," then use that as inspiration to create the body that you desire.

Without the original negative thought, you would not have had the inclination to make the change, so the negative thought is actually, a good thing. You don't want to dwell on negative thoughts, but if you stand guard at your mind, you can use them to your advantage.

Another key to happiness, is surrounding yourself with happy people. It has been said that you are the sum of your closest friends. The people that you surround yourself with, are the person that you become. I have mentioned a few times throughout the book, that my best friend of forty years, was quite different to me, so far as his outlook on life. There is nothing wrong with this. He is entitled to live his life how he chooses; as is everyone else.

The problem with the combination of my outlook and his, was that

Happiness

because they were opposites and both strong, neither one could move the other in their own direction. I would not trade the awesome forty years that we had as best mates for anything in the world, but in hindsight, I now see how I was being held back from the life that I wanted to create, just like he was being held back from the life that he wanted to create. As much as it may seem to be the case, both of us being held back, had very little to do with each other.

It is more a case of me allowing myself to be surrounded by different attitudes and mindsets to that of which I wanted to achieve and vice versa. I now choose to have those around me who support me, challenge me and hold me to a higher account. If you want to grow and achieve in life, surround yourself with people who force you to be a better person. By force, I mean that you are compelled to be a better person, because of how you were inspired by their actions.

If you want to be a professional singer, you spend time with other professional singers. Lessons and skills will rub off on you. If you want to be a great investor, I would not suggest spending too much time with people who spend all their money on lifestyle possessions, because you will feel compelled to compete with them and you will end up broke and in debt.

You must remove toxic people from your life. If these toxic people are family members, then limit your exposure to them. For most people, it is hard not to be influenced by toxic people, so the less you have them around, the less you will be influenced by them, or be dragged down by them. Toxic people want to live in a world where they can feel horrible, blame everything and everyone and have excuses as to why their life sux.

It can be heartbreaking to let go of toxic people who you love (I know firsthand), but in the long run, it is best for you and for them. You may not realise how much they are affecting you, but you will, once they are gone.

Find mentors who can guide you through life. Most truly successful people, feel compelled to give back, once they have made it. Ray Dalio, Richard Branson and Warren Buffett, all give back these days and they all say that it is the most rewarding part of their lives. I personally, have a desire to share my experience with young singers and dancers, just like I was mentored by professionals, when I started out. I also felt compelled to share the wonderful insights that I have gained through reading 280 books in one year.

This is why I also wanted to share my learnings with you in this book. For thousands of years, tribal elders shared secrets of life with the younger tribe members and this information was passed down through generations. It is something that for the most part, is lost these days. Thankfully, there is a growing movement of authors, leaders and entrepreneurs, who have embraced this way of life and shared their knowledge, so that others can benefit from it.

We live in the best time for growth and learning. The internet has allowed us to learn and develop skills in any area of our lives. If it wasn't for the internet, I would not have gained the knowledge that has allowed me to write this book. Personal development is not something that you do once. It's not a book, a seminar or an audio program. Personal development is a never-ending journey that you set off on. A journey where you constantly push yourself to be happy, be enlightened and to live according to your purpose in life.

Tony Robbins coined the phrase it in his audio series *Get the Edge*, as C.A.N.I. This stands for Constant And Never-ending Improvement. It doesn't matter how little you grow each day; as long as you grow. It could be one extra push-up, one additional dollars saved, one more page read than yesterday. As long as you're moving.

That's not to say that you don't take time to reflect, be grateful and quiet your mind. These are all part of the big picture. Whatever your journey is, is yours to decide. This book is not your bible and Tony is not your guru. Myself and any book or teacher, are merely a stepping stone along your path of discovery, happiness and fulfilment.

I've touched on many topics, but not gone into too much detail in this book. This is because I want you to get curious and discover your path and what works for you. The tools I have shared with you have changed my life, but for you they are just examples of how you too can create the life you want.

Happiness

My advice to you, is to take what you've learnt here and use this as the starting point for your own journey. Find what works for you through reading & learning and take it to the next level. Build on what I have taught you and pass it on. We stand on the shoulders of those who went before us, so it has been my pleasure to serve you and my hope that you stand on my shoulders and create your own legacy, for those who follow.

In closing, I want to share with you, a scripture that was given to me, by a friend many years ago, when I was struggling with things in my life. I didn't realise at the time, how famous this scripture was, or that it was my mother's favourite story, but when I read it, I knew right away, of its truth; despite me not being a religious person at the time. Unbeknown to me, my mother was very religious. This was something that she never pushed onto me or my siblings, but none the less, she held this poem in such high regard.

There is much debate over who the true author of this poem is, but most believe it to be the work of the late Mary Stevenson, who originally wrote the poem in 1939, when she was just fourteen years old. The poem became famous in the early 1980's when it was published and widely copied.

I want to leave you with this incredible poem, as a reminded that no matter what life throws at you, you will never walk alone.

FOOTPRINTS
(Also known as "Footprints in the Sand")

One night a man had a dream.
He dreamed he was walking along the beach with the Lord.
Across the sky flashed scenes form his life.
For each scene he noticed footprints in the sand.
Sometimes there were two sets of footprints,
Other times there were one set of footprints.
He noticed that there was only one set of footprints,
during the lowest and saddest times of his life.

CREATE THE LIFE YOU WANT

This bothered him and he questioned the Lord about it.
"Lord, you said that once I decided to follow you,
you'd walk with me all the way.
But I noticed that during the most troublesome times of my life,
there is only one set of footprints.
I don't understand why, when I needed you most,
you would leave me.

The Lord replied,
"My precious child, I love you and I would never leave you.
During your times of trial and suffering,
when you see only one set of footprints,
It was then that I carried you".

God bless.

J.D Moorea

(The Author)

Recommended Reading

I have mentioned many authors and teachers throughout this book, all of which I hope you explore and learn from. Below is a list of some of the 280 books that I read in one year. I recommend them all and hope that you enjoy them and learn from them as much as I did.

On Attitude:

- *Think and Grow Rich* – Napoleon Hill
- *Man's Search for Meaning* – Viktor E Fankl
- *The Power of Positive Thinking* – Norman Vincent Peale
- *Excuses Begone* – Dr Wayne Dyer
- *Feel the Fear and Do It Anyway* – Susan Jeffers
- *Philosophy of Successful Living* – Jim Rohn
- *The Secret* – Rhonda Byrne
- *Don't Give Up* – Paul Hanna
- *The Outsiders Edge* – Brent D Taylor
- *The Magic of Thinking Big* – David Schwartz
- *The Success Principles* – Jack Canfield
- *7 Habits of Highly Effective People* – Stephen Covey
- *The Little Guide to A Brilliant Attitude* – Bob Allwright

On Taking Action

- *How to Win Friends and Influence* People – Dale Carnegie
- *The Virgin Way* – Richard Branson
- *Screw It, Let's Do It* – Richard Branson
- *Excuses Begone* – Wayne Dyer
- *Zero Limits* - Joe Vitale
- *You Can Do It* – Paul Hanna

- *Feel the Fear and Do It Anyway* – Susan Jeffers

On Learning:

- *The Magic Ladder to Success* – Napoleon Hill
- *Better than Good* – Zig Ziglar
- *Start with Why* – Simon Sinek
- *The Power of Positive Thinking* – Norman Vincent Peale
- *The Alchemist* – Paulo Coelho
- *Change Your Questions, Change Your Life* – Marilee Adams
- *The Power of Now* – Eckhart Tolle

On Wealth:

- *Money Master the Game* – Tony Robbins
- *Unshakeable* – Tony Robbins
- *The Little Book of Investing Wisdom* – Jack C Bogle
- *Rule #1* – Phil Town
- *The Intelligent Investor* – Benjamin Graham
- *Security Analysis* – Benjamin Graham
- *Secrets of the Millionaire Mind* – T Harv Eker
- *Financial Freedom* – Suzie Orman
- *Payback Time* – Phil Town
- *Making Money* – Paul Clitheroe
- *Beating the Street* – Peter Lynch
- *It's Not About the Money* – Bob Proctor
- *One Up On Wall Street* – Peter Lynch
- *The Little Book on Value Investing* – Christopher H Browse

On Health:

- *Boundless Energy* – Deepak Chopra
- *Burn the Fat, Feed the Muscle* – Tom Venuto
- *Perfect Health* – Deepak Chopra
- *8 Weeks to Optimum Health* – Deepak Chopra

Recommended Reading

- *The Body You Deserve* (Audio Program) – Tony Robbins
- *Healthy Eating Highway* – Penny Steward
- *Zero Belly Diet* – David Zinczenko
- *The Four-Hour Body* – Tim Ferriss
- *Good Health, Good Life* – Joyce Meyer
- *Get the Edge Audio Program* (Day 4 – Pure Energy Live) – Tony Robbins

On Love:

- *Romantic Relationships* – Marianne Williamson
- *The Five Love Languages* – Gary Chapman
- *Spirit Junkie* – Gabrielle Bernstein
- *Devine Love* – Wayne Dyer
- *Attracting Love* – Tricia Brennan
- *Loving What Is* – Byron Katie
- *Get the Edge Audio Program* (Day 3 – The Power Of Relationships) – Tony Robbins

On Happiness:

- *The Gratitude Effect* – Dr John Demartini
- *Inspired Destiny* – Dr John Demartini
- *Living the Art of Allowing* – Esther and Jerry Hicks
- *Finding the Path to Joy* - Esther and Jerry Hicks
- *Manifest Your Destiny* – Wayne Dyer
- *Success and Happiness* – Andrew Matthews
- *Don't Sweat the Small Stuff* – Michael Mantel
- *Conversations with God* – Neale Donald Walsch
- *The Subtle Art of Not Giving a Fuck* – Mark Manson
- *The Celestine Prophecy* – James Redfield

Quotes

I love quotes and used to keep a foolscap folder full of thousands of awesome quotes. I have used a few throughout the book, but below are some of the ones that I had hoped to use in this book, but was unable to find a place for them.

"Don't pole vault over mouse turds." —Wayne Dyer

"Those who know, do not talk & those who talk, do not know." —Laozi

"The worst experience of your life can be the best; if you decide to use it." —Amy Morin

"Rejection can be like mulch. Dirty & smelly; but essential for growth." —Amy Morin

"Formal education will get you a job, but self-education is what will make you rich." —Jim Rohn

"You do not understand something until you can explain it to someone else so that they understand it." —Bob Proctor

"Excellence is a commitment to completion." —John Canary

"There is a season to sow & a season to reap & you don't do both in the same season." —Bob Proctor

"In every moment of your life, you have a choice. You can either be a host to God, or a hostage to ego." —Wayne Dyer

"Inner victories precede outer victories." —Stephen Covey

"God's delays are not God's denials." —Tony Robbins

www.ingramcontent.com/pod-product-compliance
Lightning Source LLC
Chambersburg PA
CBHW061648040426
42446CB00010B/1644